A
BUNCH of
Pretty Things
I Did Not
Buy

PENGUIN BOOKS
A BUNCH OF PRETTY THINGS I DID NOT BUY

Sarah Lazarovic lives
in Toronto with her
husband and two
children and a lot
of stuff.

A BUNCH of Pretty Things I Did Not Buy

Sarah Lazarovic

PENGUIN BOOKS

PENGUIN BOOKS

Published by the Penguin Group
Penguin Group (USA) LLC
375 Hudson Street
New York, New York 10014

USA | Canada | UK | Ireland | Australia | New Zealand | India | South Africa | China
penguin.com
A Penguin Random House Company

First published in Penguin Books 2014

ISBN 978-0-14-312471-9

Printed in the United States of America
1 3 5 7 9 10 8 6 4 2

FOR
Ben
and
PLUM

(who
don't
care
what
I
wear)
(unless
I look
really
weird)

contents

A BUNCH of Pretty Things I Did Not Buy

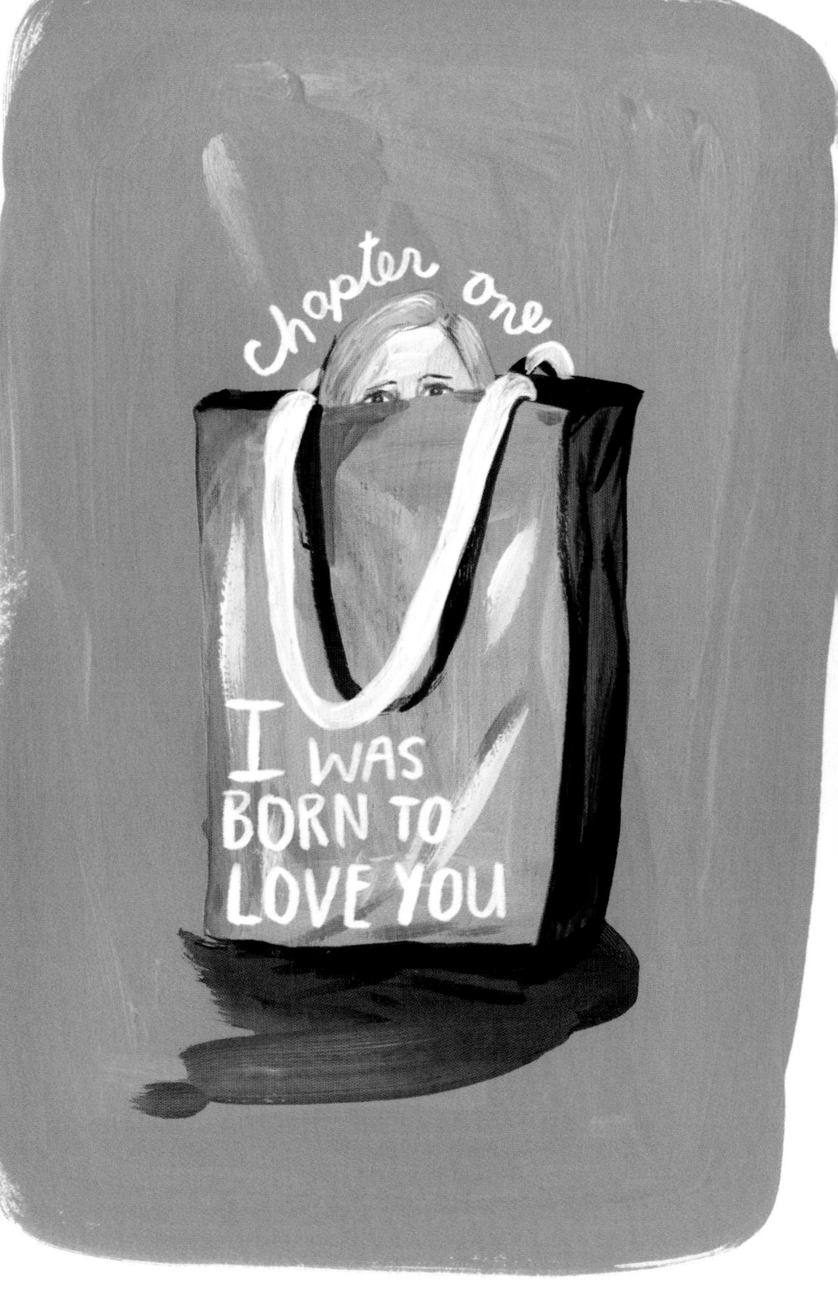
chapter one
I WAS BORN TO LOVE YOU

I WANT

How many times did I say this in my youth? A million. What did I want? A dollhouse with an elevator, puffy paints, extra large stuffed animals of dubious provenance, everything!

I don't think I wanted more than your average kid. It's just that the average kid coming of age in the late twentieth century had opportunity to gaze upon so much shiny, pretty stuff.

2

An easel would drastically improve my Quality of life.

Coordination is significantly bettered by Pink roller skates.

Connect Four is good for my brain.

Have you heard of Teddy Ruxpin? His verbal skills would no doubt improve my own.

But as toddlery screams of fleeting desire gave way to childish passions of slightly longer duration, I began to define my person by what my person wanted. I also evolved from loose whiner to targeted persuader. **3**

Boca Raton, the city I was raised in, was a pocket of wealth surrounded by poverty. I was bused to magnet schools in impoverished neighborhoods. This was the Florida public school system's way of elevating underperforming institutions. As a result, I spent my childhood feeling either sheepishly wealthy or embarrassingly poor. I became preoccupied with stuff—who had it, who didn't. My wealthy friends had fiefdoms of My Little Ponies. My lone Little Pony dreamed of companionship.

I kept my most treasured trinkets under my bathroom sink, away from the sticky fingers of my younger sisters. My pony died of scurvy.

HELD UP WITH ELASTIC BANDS FOR IDEAL HEIGHT

Mostly I coveted scrunchy socks. Friends had drawers full of them. I was allowed two pairs, but I would have gladly sacrificed a kidney for more. (Better yet, a foot; that way I'd instantly have four pairs.)

6

There wasn't much to do in suburbia. I became a weekend mall rat, apportioning my allowance to flowered boxers from the Gap that I wore as shorts (horrors!). I could name every store in the mall, and opine disdainfully on which ones didn't deserve to be there.

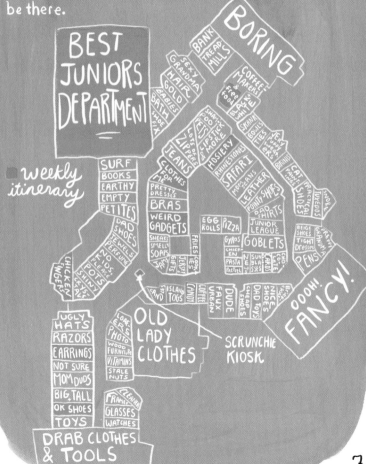

7

Visual identity in pre-Internet suburbia was hard to come by. It required work of a sort not necessary today. If you wanted two-tone brogues because you were in an adolescent ska phase, you had to beg your mother to drive you forty-five minutes to the strange store in the depressing strip mall where you thought you might procure a pair.

South Florida was then a strange mix of bland suburbia and unchecked kitsch. Now it's almost exclusively bland suburbia. On weekends I cultivated my appreciation for tchotchkes by going to the Thunderbird Swap Shop with my grandmother. I delighted in the cheap, tacky plastic trinkets on offer. It was all crap. But it was bizarre crap my friends and schoolmates didn't have.

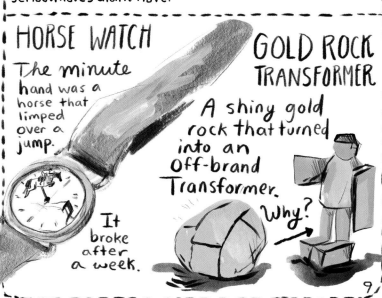

HORSE WATCH

The minute hand was a horse that limped over a jump.

It broke after a week.

GOLD ROCK TRANSFORMER

A shiny gold rock that turned into an off-brand Transformer.

Why?

9

In seventh grade my family went to London and Paris. The beautiful things blew my mind. I brought home a pair of green Doc Martens with a tiny, chintzy pattern of fruit. They invoked awe from friends and strangers. I wore them for years.

With high school came the freedom of mobility. My friends and I would drive to Miami or Fort Lauderdale for thrift shops and record stores. We'd finally discovered the cool stuff—punk albums at Uncle Sam's Music in South Beach, used old-man corduroy slacks at Howard's in Lake Worth. Even though I'd abandoned my beloved mall, I was still a girl consumed by stuff, adding miles to the odometer in search of the perfect vintage T-shirt.

HOW TO PICK THE PERFECT mechanic SHIRT:

1. NO GROSS STAINS

2. MINIMAL MUSTINESS

3. GOOD NAME TAG

Later in life, when I'd meet really well-read people or fantastic musicians, I'd wonder where my youth had gone. All those hours tooling around in search of the thing that could make me amazing. I should have been practicing my violin.

If I look back upon all this time as frivolous consumerism, I get really depressed. So instead I'll rebrand it as "identity formation." I was deciding I didn't want to be a samey-samey Gap girl. I was cultivating the me I wanted to present to others.

PAINT–SPLATTERED SHIRT WITH OLD-MAN CORDUROYS

SPAghetti Straps + SHORT SHORTS

MOM'S OLD DRESS and WINTER BOOTS

Trying really hard to look like I don't care.

Infuriating my dad.

Boots in Florida = Ridiculous.

People often decry any attention to clothes as vacuous. Sure, if it's all you care about. But how can trying to say something about who you are and what you believe be totally empty? And besides, we all have to get dressed each day.

ALL black

Bubby's MUUMUU & clogs

OLD SHIRT AND CORDS. Again.

Brief and lazy attempt at Goth look.

I'm an artist.

I really don't care. I mean it!

And what of the ill-defined distinction between fashion and shopping? In childhood we create fashion with very little shopping (except you, Suri Cruise). We have neither access to shops nor cash flow, so we have to be creative.

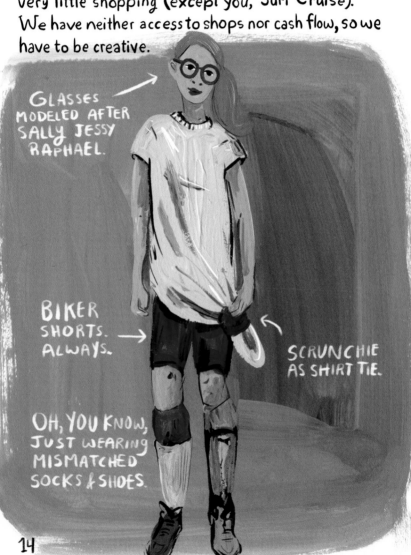

GLASSES MODELED AFTER SALLY JESSY RAPHAEL.

BIKER SHORTS. ALWAYS. →

SCRUNCHIE AS SHIRT TIE.

OH, YOU KNOW, JUST WEARING MISMATCHED SOCKS & SHOES.

It's a stretch to say that limitation begets style, but the improvisation that stricture inspires can lead to some wonderful dressing.

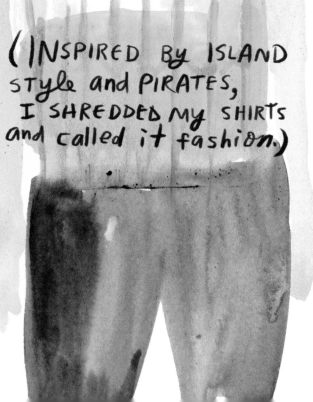

(INSPIRED BY ISLAND style and PIRATES, I SHREDDED MY SHIRTS and called it fashion.)

Unless you're born with outsize character and unfathomable beauty, you spend at least 67% of your adolescence fretting about what you look like. You spend the rest of the time eating Doritos and ogling teen pop stars with remarkably good skin.

If you're of normal constitution, you cry a lot. Covering your jeans in safety pins tells the world you're a badass. And who would deny a growing creature that small protection against the cruelties of life?

So we are born to love clothes for the safety they grant us. For the way they make us feel. For the way they make our butt look. And there's nothing wrong with that.

An aside: Growing up, there were always those girls whose mothers dressed them, immaculately and adorably, in the latest trends, inspiring envy among their peers and garnering them instant popularity.

I got to know one of these girls later in high school, and she was an indifferent and uninspired dresser. I wondered if these moms had done their kids a disservice. I may have looked ridiculous 98% of the time, but I was free to dress however I pleased. I was free to develop my own tragic style.

19

What's interesting is how little brands played into it. I'm not that old, and yet the landscape has changed. Yes, I coveted shirts with wee horses on them, etc., but when I worked as a sleepaway camp counselor, I was amazed at the way my ten-year-old charges referred to their belongings with branded savvy.

Our formative fashion is a piece of our formative everything. We're shaping the thinkers, doers, and wearers we will someday be. In some ways, we buy thoughtlessly in youth (buy me something, anything, just buy buy buy!), but we also begin to establish how to shop on a budget (I will have to save my allowance for three weeks if I really want these puke-green scrunchy socks).

21

It's important stuff. And it's the stuff that our memory holds fast to for the rest of our lives. I remember the beautiful Sabatino snakeskin party shoes my mom always wanted me to wear. I remember the red Converse high-tops, the eyelet flower girl dress. And I try to forget the bedazzled hot-pink dress suit (but the shoulder pads live on in my nightmares).

22

CHAPTER *two*

Disposable Income, Disposable Underwear

When I finally got to university I had a shopping awakening. I had a budget, and it was up to me whether I was going to allocate my funds toward late-night pizza or fancy coffees or clothes.

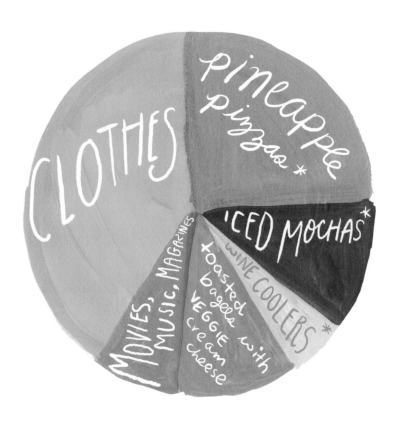

CLOTHES

pineapple pizzas *

'ICED MOCHAS*

WINE COOLERS *

toasted bagels with veggie cream cheese

MOVIES, MUSIC, MAGAZINES

*I know.

2-ply Sandpaper RECYCLED Sandpaper

Smelly Quilted Barbie

Moving away from home, every purchase was a revelation. Do I buy skim milk because my parents did, or 2% because it's pleasantly indulgent? Do I shop at the twenty-four-hour Walmart or the university health co-op? Every choice was a defining moment.

It's these maiden steps in personal consumption that begin to define us. But how not to go off track if our particular moment of consumer liberation comes just when everything is so plentiful, so accessible, and so cheap? It's a recipe for overindulgence. For hauling. For buying as many rayon dresses as a crisp $20 bill will afford you.

Get anything good?

No, but I got a lot.

THINGS THAT GO THROUGH YOUR MIND WHEN YOU'RE DANCING ON THE STAGE AT A GAY CLUB in A STRIP MALL WHILE WEARING A SEQUINED UNITARD:

I'M ONLY young once.
THANK Heavens I'M ONLY YOUNG once.

THE "70S MUST HAVE BEEN an itchy DECADE.

AM I A FAG HAG?

IS THE TERM FAG HAG INSULTING OR JUST STUPID?

II COULD GO FOR SOME PIZZA!

II COULD ALSO GO FOR SOME ICE CREAM.

"COME on EILEEN" is the best song IN the WORLD.

SHOULD I HAVE ANOTHER Malibu & PINEAPPLE?

RUNNING MAN? yes? no? yes!

This opportunity for experimentation is fantastic because you can know what it feels like to wear a purple sequin onesie. And horrible because you can know what it feels like to wear a purple sequin onesie.

TOO MANY PAIRS OF SLUTTY UNDERWEAR

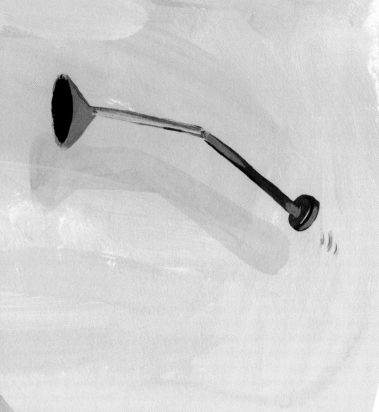

One of the grossest things I've ever seen was the garbage room the day I moved out of my freshman dorm. It was a shrine to waste, to hastily bought and easily discarded crap: cheap halogen lamps snapped in two, clothes, furniture—the detritus of a year of misguided shopping.

It's a truism that young people need financial education. But don't they need shopping education as well?

THESE SHOES ARE VERY EXPENSIVE, YET THEY'RE MADE FROM POOR-QUALITY MATERIALS IN TERRIBLE CONDITIONS.

BUT THEY'RE SO SHINY!

When I was twenty clothes weren't as cheap. In a dozen years, H&M's prices have made the Gap's seem like thievery.

Top Secret cap, $39.99

Cat Burglar top, $54.99

Jewel thief skimmers, $59.99

And if all the clothes are made in the same sweatshops, what accounts for their price disparities?

H&M, $20 — MADE in CHINA

GAP, $60 — MADE in CHINA

J.Crew $125 — MADE IN CHINA

CLUB MONACO, $220 — MADE IN CHINA

What's more, the fashion cycle has quickened so much that if you take a nap you can miss a season.

FALL

LATE FALL

DENYING IT'S WINTER

ADMITTING IT'S WINTER

SPRING

MORE SPRING

RESORT

TACKY, ALL-INCLUSIVE RESORT

STAY-CATION

SUMMER

MORE SUMMER, PLEASE

NO IDEA

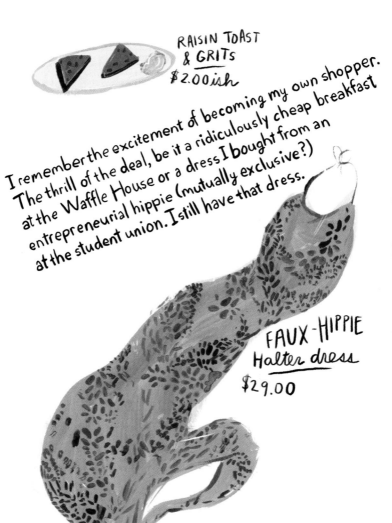

RAISIN TOAST
& GRITS
$2.00ish

I remember the excitement of becoming my own shopper.
The thrill of the deal, be it a ridiculously cheap breakfast
at the Waffle House or a dress I bought from an
entrepreneurial hippie (mutually exclusive?)
at the student union. I still have that dress.

FAUX-HIPPIE
Halter dress
$29.00

INCENSE HOLDER
& noxious incense
sticks
can't remember   33

This excitement, however, was intermittently muted by a nascent shopper's conscience. Yes, I could buy freely, but if I purchased wantonly or wastefully, the guilt was my own to bear.

TIME SPENT WEARING GUNNE SAX dress: 2 hours

TIME SPENT TRYING ON GUNNE SAX DRESS and then deciding not to wear it: 6,000 hours

TIME spent feeling guilty about not wearing Gunne Sax dress: 9,247 hours

It's unfortunate that shopping becomes synonymous with guilt and frivolity so early in life. But without a proper handbook for how to buy, I learned through my mistakes: foolish purchases, wasted money, self-recrimination.

When things got so cheap that it became mindless to buy them (2005?), I wondered if someone was going to realize it had all been a mistake and come charge me the real price for the $7 flapper dress I got at H&M. I'm still waiting.

36

Years later, it hit me that everything was too cheap and too copious and too thoughtless. But even then, only in that "yes, but whatever" way.

REST-OF-LIFE TO-DO LIST:

- FINISH COLLEGE
- FIND BOYFRIEND
- FIGURE OUT WHAT TO DO WITH LIFE
- SMOOTHIES
- EXERCISE
- CHOCOLATE
- TAXES
- VISIT SLOVENIA
- STOP BUYING SWEATSHOP CLOTHES (if time permits)

For the record, after a short dalliance with whole milk, I now buy 1% organic. And I still have my unitard.

Unitards
Rave pants
kneesocks
tutus

CHAPTER three

~~A~~ ~~FEW~~ ~~WORDS~~ ~~ON~~ MINIMALISM

After a brief stint at a university where girls wore shorts with the university's name on the bum, I went traveling.

I wanted to slough off my former life.
I also wanted to fill a small backpack
with just a few perfect, dreamy things.

It took me years to manage this feat.

2004

2006

2008

2010

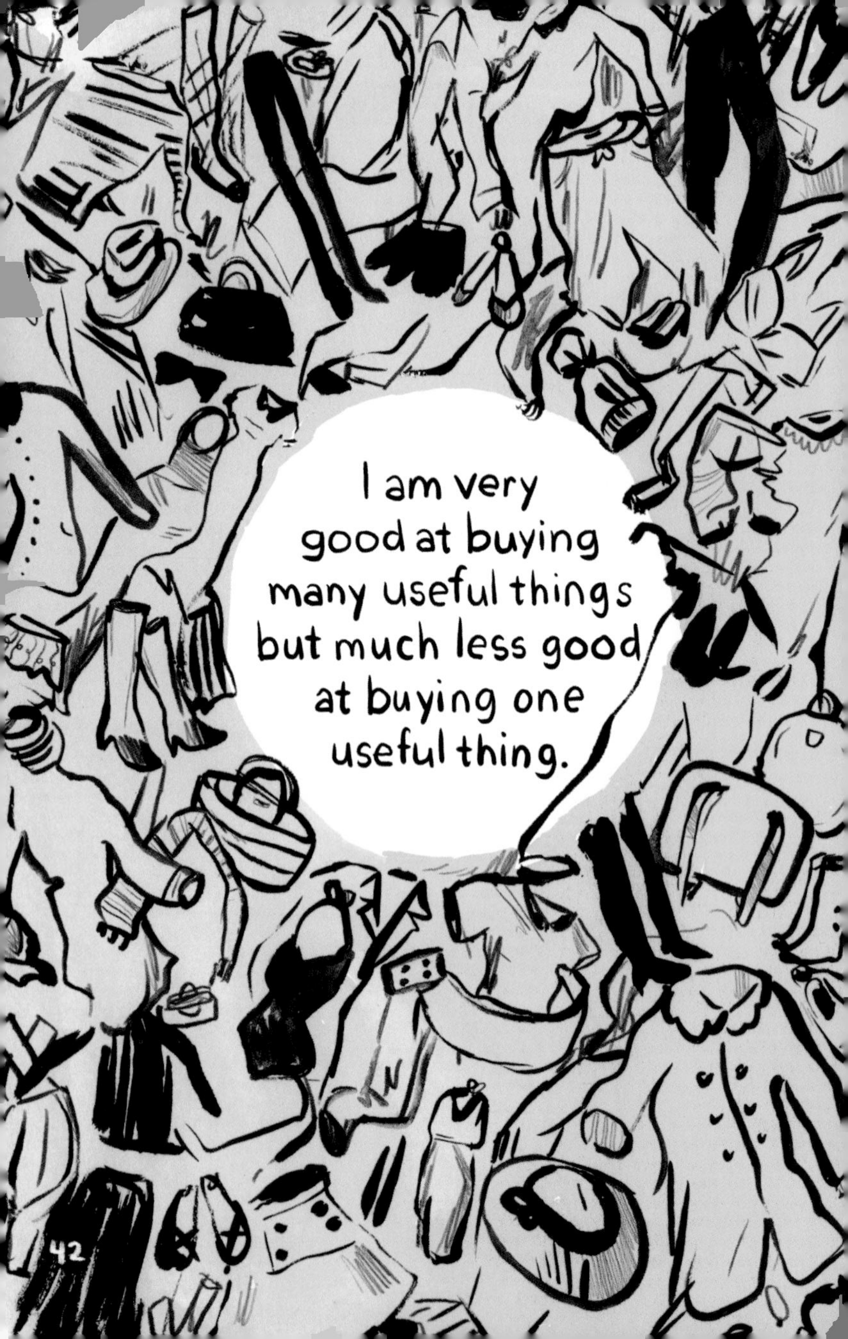
I am very good at buying many useful things but much less good at buying one useful thing.

When I look at design-porny pics of minimal, Eames-chaired lofts, I covet the nothingness. The extreme, impossible simplicity. **Counter**-intuitively, the minimal impulse inspires consumption. I have too much crap. I need more of less.

THE EYE goes HERE.

↑ BUT IT'S really aBOUT ← THIS. →
↓

I subscribe to this false tautology even as I'm completely aware of doing so. Buying to stop the buying.

amazon

Shop by Department ▾ Search All ▾ *minimalism* go

Shopping Cart

Items to buy now

Minimalism: Live a Meaningful Life - Joshua Fields Millburn, Ryan Nicodemus
Paperback
In Stock
Eligible for FREE Super Saver Shipping
☐ This will be a gift (Learn more)
Delete · Save for later

Price $11.53
You save: $3.47 (23%)

Quantity 2

The price and availability of items at Amazon are subject to change. Do you have a gift card or promotional code?

Customers Who Bought Items in Your Cart Also Bought :

MAXIMALISM
★★★ (2)
$15.50
Add to Cart

STUFF
★★★★★ (59)
$7.19
Add to Cart

MORE ON MINIMALISM
★★★ (7)
$6.27
Add to Cart

STILL MORE ON MINIMALISM
★★ (3)
$6.27
Add to Cart

44

Buying the perfect
classic flats to wear
always, always, always.

(Maybe just two pairs.)

And what of the magazine features where impossibly glamorous people tell you how to pack just five items of clothing for a trip?

In her book *The Beauty Experiment*, author Phoebe Baker Hyde writes about the perfect collection. "I give you an amalgamated version of the Must-Have List: little black dress, crisp white shirt, lightweight cashmere cardigan, perfect dark jeans, classic pumps, trench coat, pencil skirt, all-occasion bag, selection of good T-shirts, ballet flats, fitted blazer, fancy scarf, good suit, black slacks, knee-high boots, statement necklace, lace bra, 'dress' pajamas, and khaki pants."

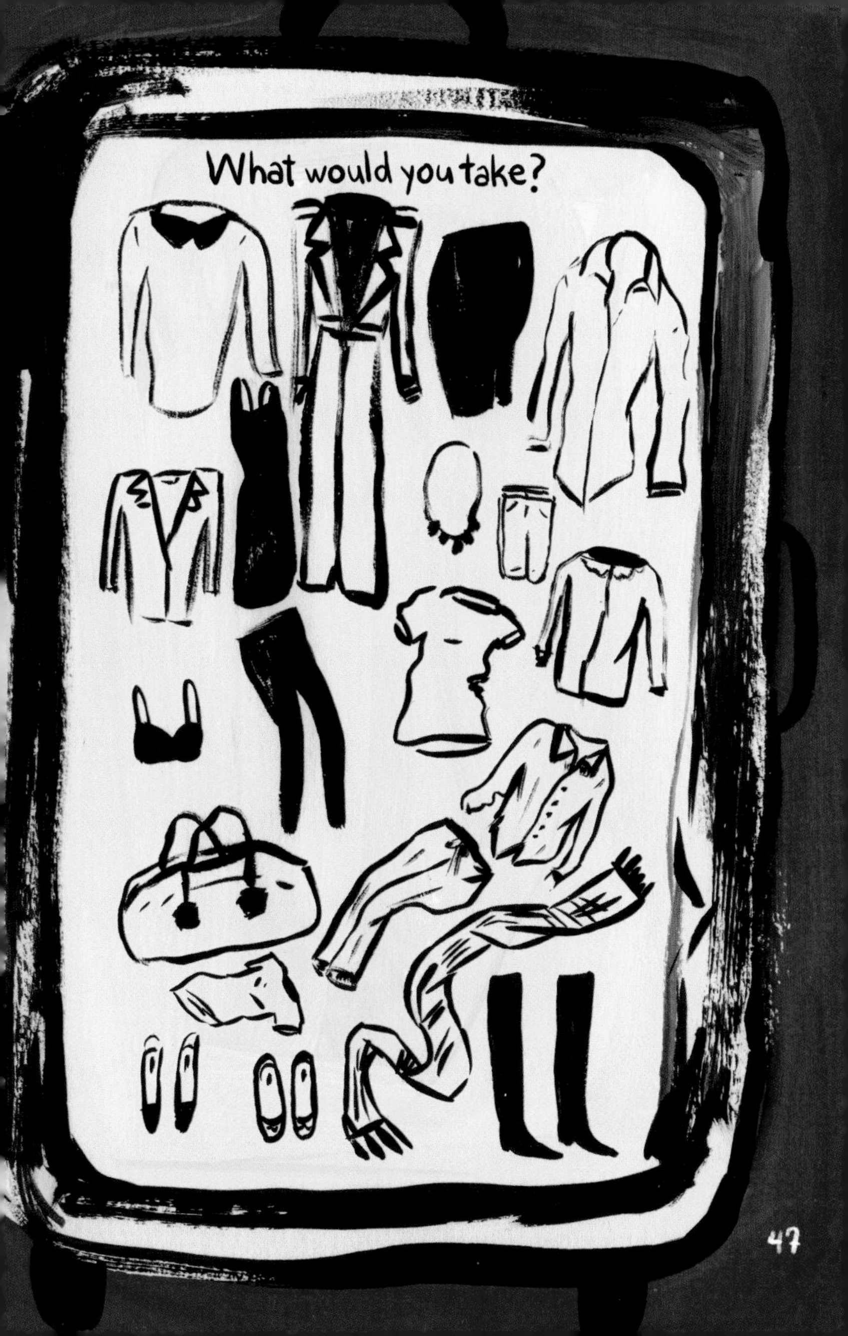
What would you take?

Minimalism is expensive. To live with beautiful austerity you have to be able to buy anything you could ever need. That's why minimalists are usually reformed dot-com billionaires.

MODERNIST CUBE HOUSE
$7,349,625.99 + tax

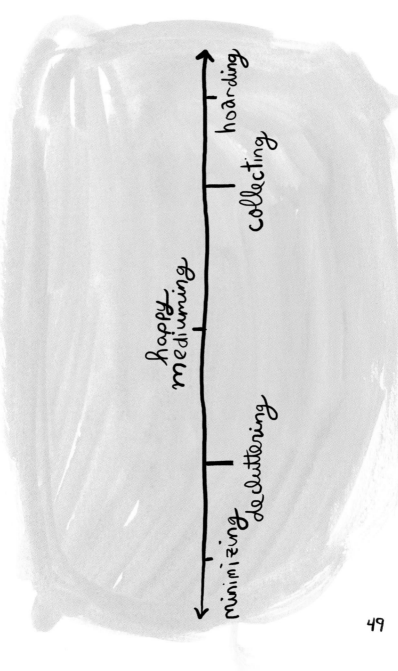

hoarding

collecting

happy mediuming

decluttering

minimizing

49

When I start examining the latest minimalist gem,
I reprimand myself. But it's in my nature.
As a kid, I coveted those pants that could be
turned into shorts with a few zips.

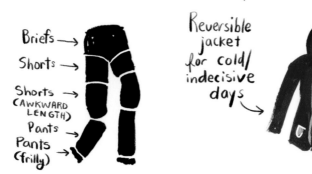

Briefs →
Shorts →
Shorts → (AWKWARD LENGTH)
Pants →
Pants → (frilly)

Reversible jacket for cold/ indecisive days →

For an embarrassingly long time, my Swiss Army
knife was my most prized possession (a tiny little thing
that can do so much).

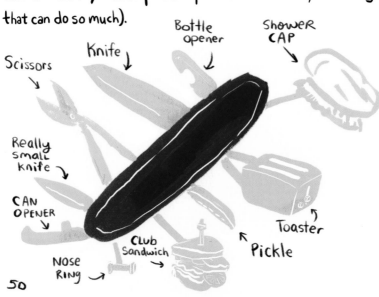

Scissors
Knife ↓
Bottle opener ↓
Shower CAP →

Really small knife →

CAN OPENER ↓

Club Sandwich →

NOSE RING →

Pickle ←

Toaster ↖

I own a pair of sandals with retractable wheels (in case I'm at the beach and feel like a skate).

EFFECTIVE neither as sandal nor skate.

Pert Plus was pretty much invented for me... until I discovered Dr. Bronner's.

THINGS YOU CAN DO WITH DR. BRONNER'S:

- Brush teeth
- Wash clothes
- Shampoo dog
- Shave
- Clean counters
- Polish wood

- Wash dishes
- End poverty*
- Remove wrinkles
- Broker peace in the middle east
- Break sound barrier
- Make chopped liver
- SQUINT (packaging text is really small)

* Kidding, alas.

51

In childhood I could love a shirt to shreds.
And keep loving it until it became indecent.
This love would eradicate the need for other
clothes. Why would I wear any other shirt when
this was the most perfect shirt of all time?

Zephyrhills is a popular
brand of bottled water
in Florida. Trailer parks
and see-through shirts
are also popular in
Florida.

It's healthy to appreciate one's clothes, but knowing what you like does not make you a fashion designer. Once, I sketched my perfect dress and had a seamstress create it twice over.

The dresses didn't hang properly. And they pilled. I gave up on them. It was hubris to think I could manufacture my perfect uniform so easily. I didn't know a stitch.

I do, however, have three of the same Banana Republic dress. I've had them for years and never tire of their easy cut. I've cycled through them, uniform style, in times of flagging sartorial strength. They never let me down. They're the workdresses of my wardrobe.

Jazzercizing

BERRY PICKING

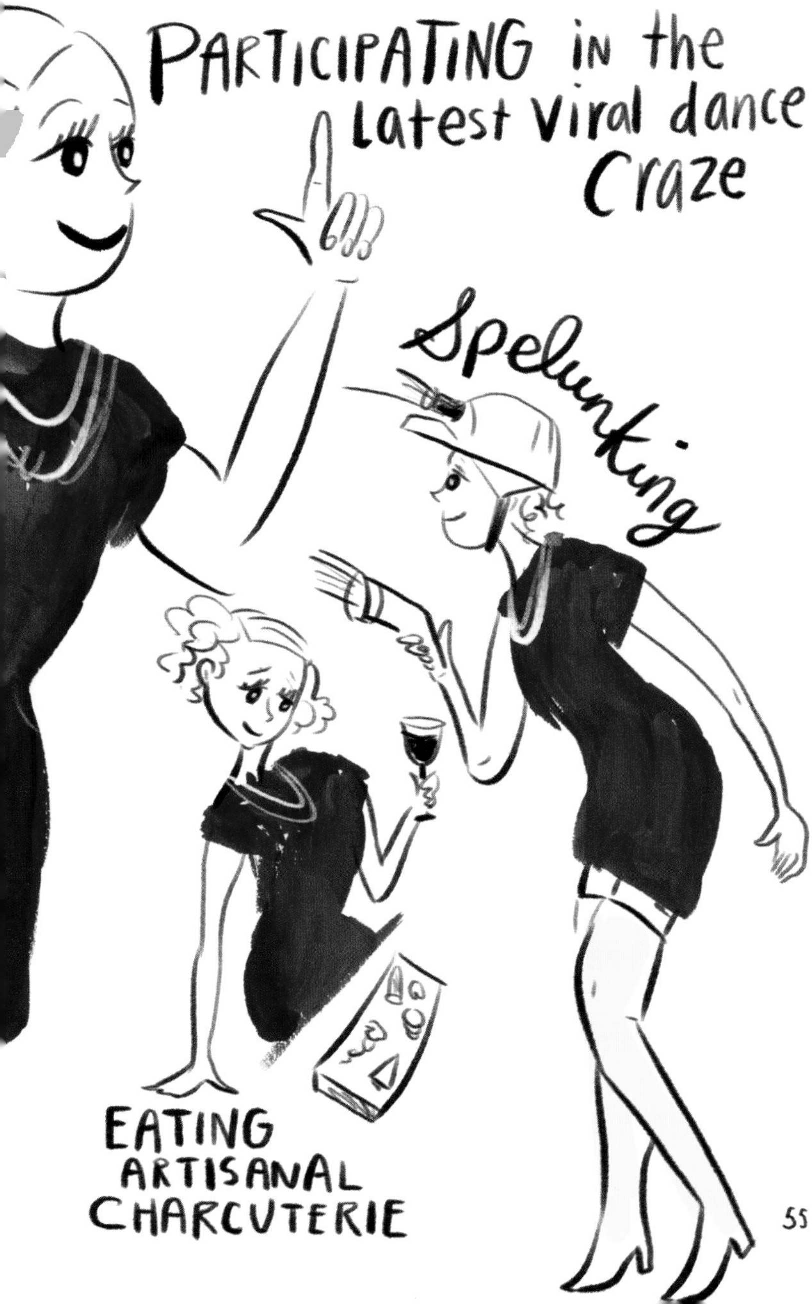
PARTICIPATING in the latest viral dance craze
Spelunking
EATING ARTISANAL CHARCUTERIE

My grandfather bought in bulk when he liked something. When he died, we found three pairs of identical gray New Balance sneakers still in boxes in his closet.

Growing up, my mum had the same Bass jazz oxfords in four colors.

I hated them all equally.

But the person who took uniform dress to minimal
excess was an art director I worked for. He was a
handsome French Canadian with tousled hair,
impeccable white dress shirts, perfect jeans, and
black leather ankle boots. He had two white shirts.
He washed one each day and wore the other one.
For a while I searched for a uniform to make so
dazzlingly my own. I'm still looking for it. 57

Bubby's
vintage
Pumps

Mom's
reversible
silk Mandarin
Jacket

Purse mom
got for her
sweet 16

Bubby's
duster

Charm bracelet
Grampa brought
back from China
in 1967

As I age I get closer to minimalized refinement.
But this is due as much to narrowing taste as it is
to power of will. At the very least, I'm wary of the
new thing that promises to alleviate the need for all
the old things. I just want to love the old things.

CHapter four

A Bunch of Pretty Things I Did Not Buy

In 2006 I didn't buy any clothes. I felt I was buying absentmindedly, sauntering into a boutique and walking out with a "find." In 2012 I decided to not shop again, after noticing I was buying too much crap on the Internet. It's not that I'm a crazy shopaholic*—I'm just really good at finding amazing stuff to buy: Amazing stuff to buy that I totally do not need. Except for that adorable sweater.

*GROSS WORD ALERT

cream/Navy Crew Neck Knit
Breton jumper, SAINT James,
£85.00

In the half-dozen years since my last shopping diet the Internet has become much more sophisticated. I can find the exact thing I covet within seconds, order it within minutes, and pay for it for days.

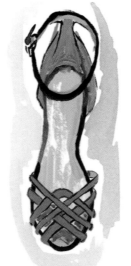

Jelly sandals, Zara, $50.00

The Internet quickens
the pace of shopping.
Instead of that magical
feeling of happening upon
something I've long wanted,
I feel anxious.
The immediacy of the
find makes me feel
I need to purchase
equally swiftly.

Enfield, Bass, $79.00

I can drill down to
find exactly what I like.
And the Internet responds.
If I look at something
once, it teases me for
weeks on end.
"Hey dork, stop being
so coy. Buy this dress,"
it shouts, from a box
to the left of the
serious article about
genetically modified
kumquats I've been trying
to absorb.

Random
Pintevest dress

I wanted a leather backpack satchel for a dozen years, but couldn't find one. Once, I even tried to hack my own, sewing crude straps onto a bag. Now I have my pick, but the profusion of choices only puts me off.

Leather backpack satchel,
golden Ponies, $120.⁰⁰

The act of not shopping, however contrived, has been a willful barricade against the flow of stuff that comes at me.

If I don't impose a rule, I buy unthinkingly, neither caring for nor truly appreciating the mint-green saddle shoes that arrive with a thwack on my porch step.

Zurich, Fluevog, $206.50

It's the endless stream of stuff that both dazzles and disgusts. On Pinterest I have to avert my eyes from the parade of pretty-page after page of effortlessly obtainable crap.

Pinterest

73

I really like Virginia Johnson's wispy tunics. But there's something vulgar about a $300 beach caftan.

Long, slim caftan,
Parachute gray,
Virginia Johnson, $295.⁰⁰

Every once in a while
my rules bug the hell
out of me. I see a dress
that makes me imagine
the million lives I could
lead in it. I worry I'll
never see something
so perfect again.
Then I remember a dress
in my closet that looks
pretty similar.

Summer dress
with cross-strap
bodice, Asos,
$53.02

At age twenty-five,
if you've grown
neither wider nor lumpier,
you have a clothes palette.
Though I'm sick of my
wide-legged floral jeans
right now, I know I'll
swing back to them.
Much to my husband's
embarrassment.

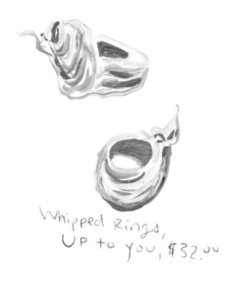

Whipped Rings,
Up to you, $32.00

I know enough to
know I'm fickle,
that I'll cycle back
from abject dismissal
to fervent love.
Which explains why
my turban is dusty.

Vulture Dress,
Birds of North America,
$164.00

It's perhaps impossible to give up shopping forever, but when I read that the average American buys sixty-eight items of clothing per year, I spit up a pair of neon jeggings. Sixty-eight new things? Was America's closet burned to the ground in a freak, fast-fashion fire?

High-Waist
Sailor shorts, Arden B.,
$49.00

83

I've experimented with all kinds of stricture, from having a seamstress sew me perfect black dresses* to trying to pare my wardrobe down to a daily uniform. What I've learned: Buying or making the perfect dress will not banish desire, or necessarily even simplify dressing.

* See chapter 3, page 53.

Valentina Dress,
Dolce Vita, $275.⁰⁰

Before I gave up shopping, I bought a beautiful, expensive dress. I imagine it's made by a cute girl in Montreal who has to charge a certain price to keep herself in coffee, cigarettes, and organic cotton. She has a dreamy, indie-rock boyfriend and a dreamy, indie-rock loft studio.

Hint cross-over
glitter Sandals,
TOPSHOP, £50.00

For the price of one indie-rock dress, I can buy ten sweatshop-rock dresses, but part of maturing is realizing I don't want to be a glutton for rayon. "Quality, not quantity," "MileEnd not Made in Bangladesh," yada yada yada— Stab me with a high-minded sewing needle.

Sleeveless low-cut dress
shirt with Bow, Betina Lou,
$120.⁰⁰

Quality isn't taught.*
Few parents instruct their kids
in the ways of button widths and
hems. When people go on about
the poor quality of high-street
chain garb, I feign understanding.
I've never had an H&M
dress expire prematurely.
Which makes abstaining
tougher. Why do I have
to give up cheaply made goods
that work? 1. Because I can't
see the parts of the process
that don't work. 2. Because
I'm looking for quality
that lasts a lifetime.

*See chapter 7, page 148.

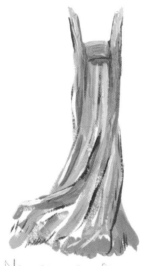

Nouveau souffle.
Cotélac, ƒ 122,50

The neat thing about resistance
is the freedom it grants.
I don't browse or examine
sartorial specimens. The time
I used to spend running my
fingers across fabrics is now
apportioned to other activities.
Valuable activities like tweeting.
And making fun of Twitter.

Mineral Necklace,
Beklina, $75.⁰⁰

Which doesn't mean I've stopped caring about dressing. I've just stopped caring about dressing in so many different things. A scarf can do so much... but it can only do so much.

BAthing beauty
oNe-piece in
Blue velvet,
ModCloth, $89.99

The occasional pieces I pine for become like paintings in a gallery. I don't need to own them to appreciate them. I don't need to wear them to appreciate them. I wouldn't look good in a Rothko anyway. It would totally wash me out.

Nanette Asymmetric
Dress, Anthropologie,
$188.00

TWO FINAL THINGS

People often ask me how not to shop. They express sentiments along the lines of, "OMG, I could never do that." I'm not a girl with unshakable willpower. I'm the girl who eats the entire pint of ice cream, the girl who plans to run twenty laps but settles for six and a half. So anyone can do it.

Also, some people need new clothes. No shame in that. Shapes change. Jobs require finery. If your work demands you don trendy, cleavage-y dresses, you need to buy trendy, cleavage-y dresses. (You might also need a new job.) SO DON'T FEEL GUILTY, you beautiful evolving person, you.

chapter five

Toward an IDEAL Home

As we get old and buy houses, yurts, and Airstream trailers, our material interest gets reallocated. I'm not completely indifferent to clothes now. I just have a garage to clean, and vintage schoolhouse lamps to source. Where once I was content to affix wrinkly concert posters to my walls, now a large chunk of my budget goes to housewares, a category of items I didn't know existed until I was twenty-seven.

But how to apply the spirit of not shopping to an empty house? Or worse, a house filled only with the garbage you could afford in your youth? The obvious answer is to buy things that last.

101

The problem with buying things to last is that taste and budget rarely inhabit the same space and time on one's home-shopping continuum,

Except for the very fortunate few who are blessed with lasting taste and great wealth.

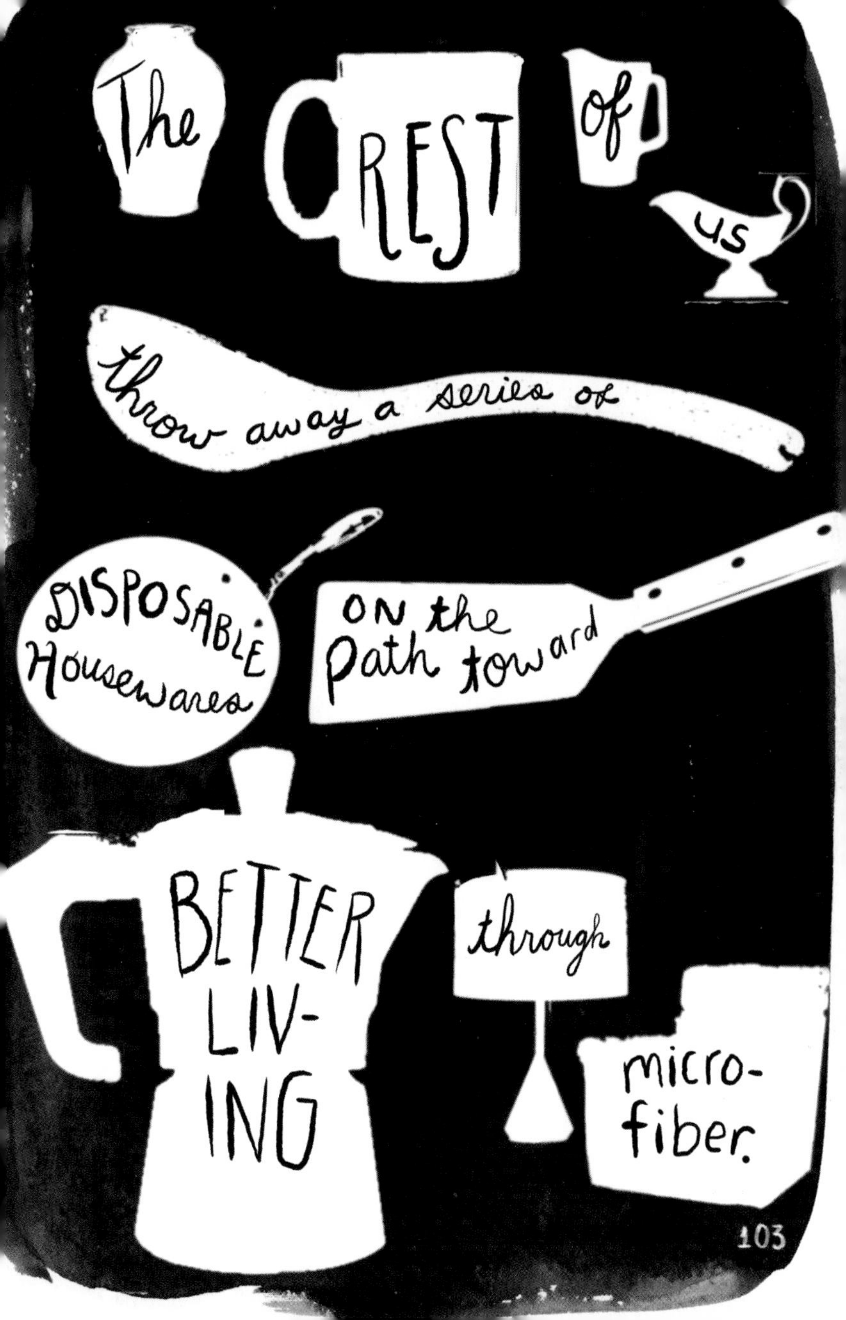
The
REST
of
us
throw away a series of
DISPOSABLE Housewares
ON the path toward
BETTER LIV-ING
through
micro-fiber.

The furniture I've purchased in my life could fill a shipping container. I've contributed to the creation of 7,249 tons of particleboard.*

*Completely unscientific yet totally accurate calculation.

But what college student can spring for a proper mattress? We buy what our means allow at each stage of life, instead of buying for life when our means allow.

I remember outfitting an entire collegiate apartment at Ikea in a few minutes. I went from room to room, picking out the space I'd live in for the next two years in less time than it takes to watch a sitcom. I also ate a pretzel.

The ability to devote absolutely no time or energy to our living spaces is both wonderful and awful. Wonderful because we get to say things like Fjlark. Awful because the Fjlark falls apart after a few years.

As I divest myself of compressed sawdust, I'm weighed down by the waste. Unlike my grandmother's solid wood furniture, this stuff doesn't last. It has the life span of an ice sculpture.

But what's the solution? Should I have slept on the floor until such time as I could afford the natural mattress and teak headboard?

I've worked out a formula:

PURCHASE=TIME+RESEARCH-ALLEN KEYS

What comes into my house now must be mulled, researched, deliberated upon.

And yet I amortize with the best of them to justify big-ticket purchases.

ONE COUCH @ $3,000.⁰⁰=

a fuck a sit for 8.2 years (or 4.1 years, for two bums).

DEAL.

110

When

need SOME-thing

SEARCH

FOR

IT

used

FIRST.

When I need something I search for it used first.

But again, I'm not immune to the cushiony call of the beautiful piece.

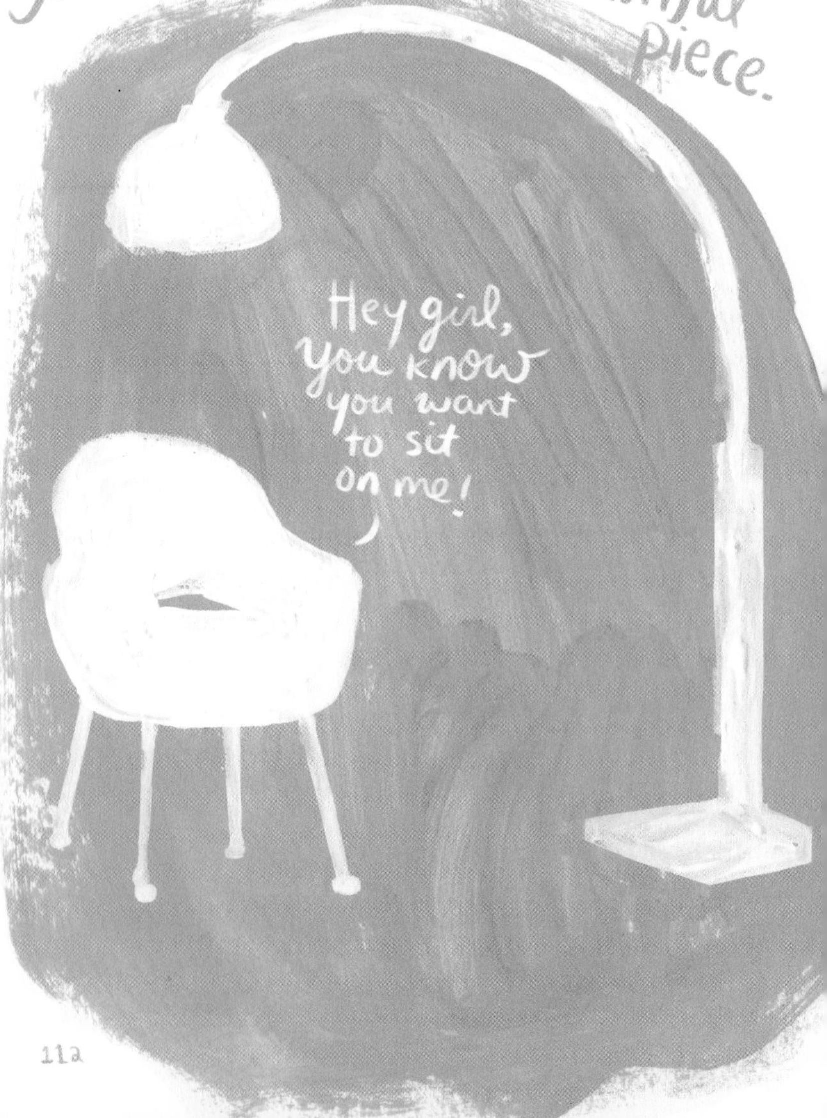
Hey girl, you know you want to sit on me!

And I worry that just as
the thirty-year-old me looks
upon her twenty-year-old
taste with self-loathing,
the forty-year-old me may
find her thirty-year-old
taste untenable.

After all, isn't that how
boomers end up with
rooms of neotraditional
fuggery?

A home needs to be
a cozy haven,

but spend too much
time cozying and
there's not enough
time left
for living.

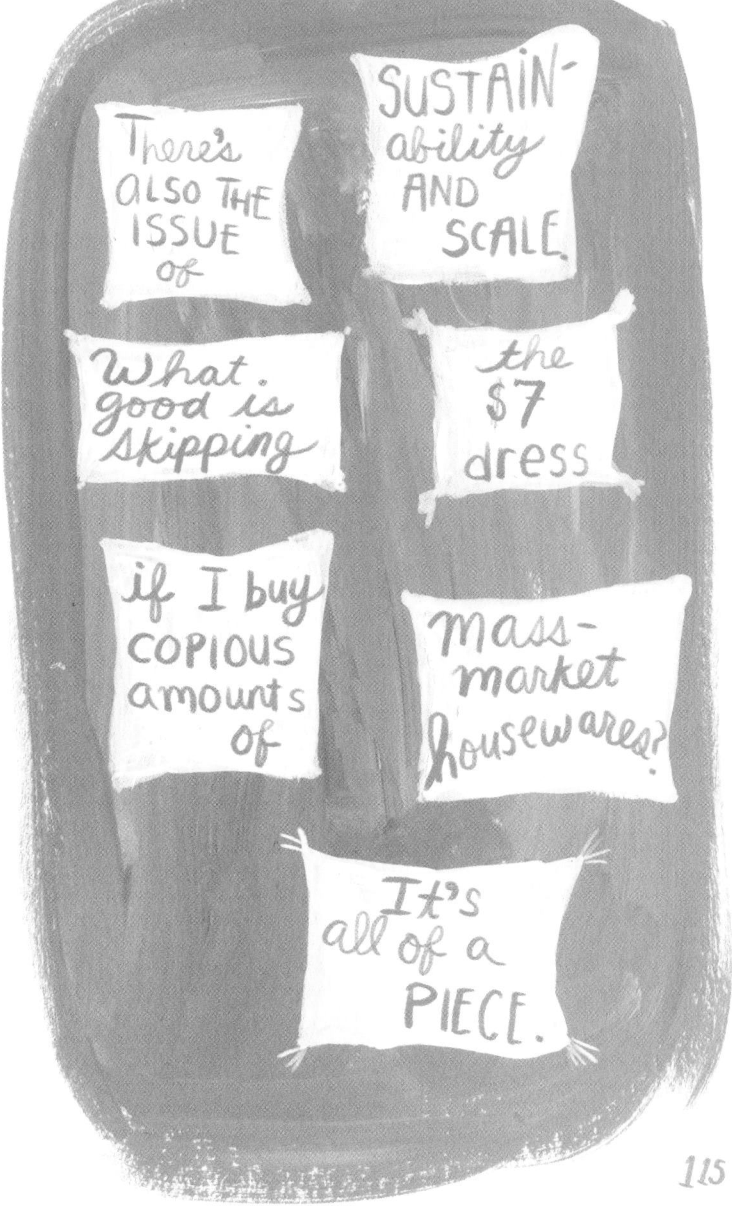
There's also the issue of
SUSTAIN-ability AND SCALE.
What good is skipping
the $7 dress
if I buy COPIOUS amounts of
mass-market housewares?
It's all of a PIECE.

A loophole:
I justify unnecessary
indulgences* as

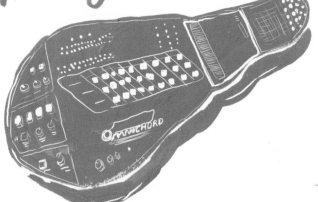

"tools for
Creativity."

*OMNICHORD for sale.
$200 OBO.
contact: @sarahLazarovic

When I was younger I never threw anything away. My catchphrase was, "I can use that for something."

Now, there are no
escape clauses.
 I have to make
a case for everything.
And a place, too.

Stuff

things

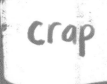
crap

crap
annex

CHAPTER six

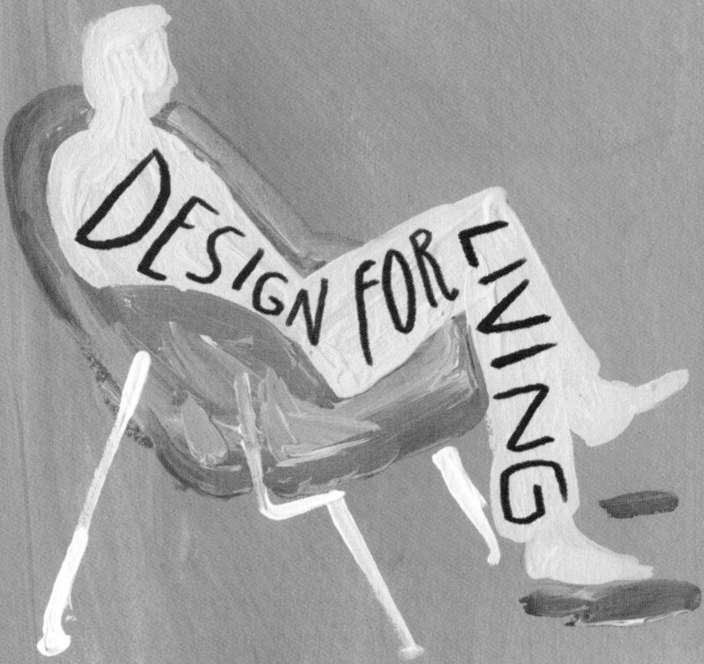
DESIGN FOR LIVING

It's small pleasures that make us most happy. Science backs me up on this one, and personal experience confirms it.

Writing recently in *Scientific American*, Sonja Lyubomirsky says that one of the most effective ways to achieve happiness through money is to spend on small pleasures instead of big-ticket items.

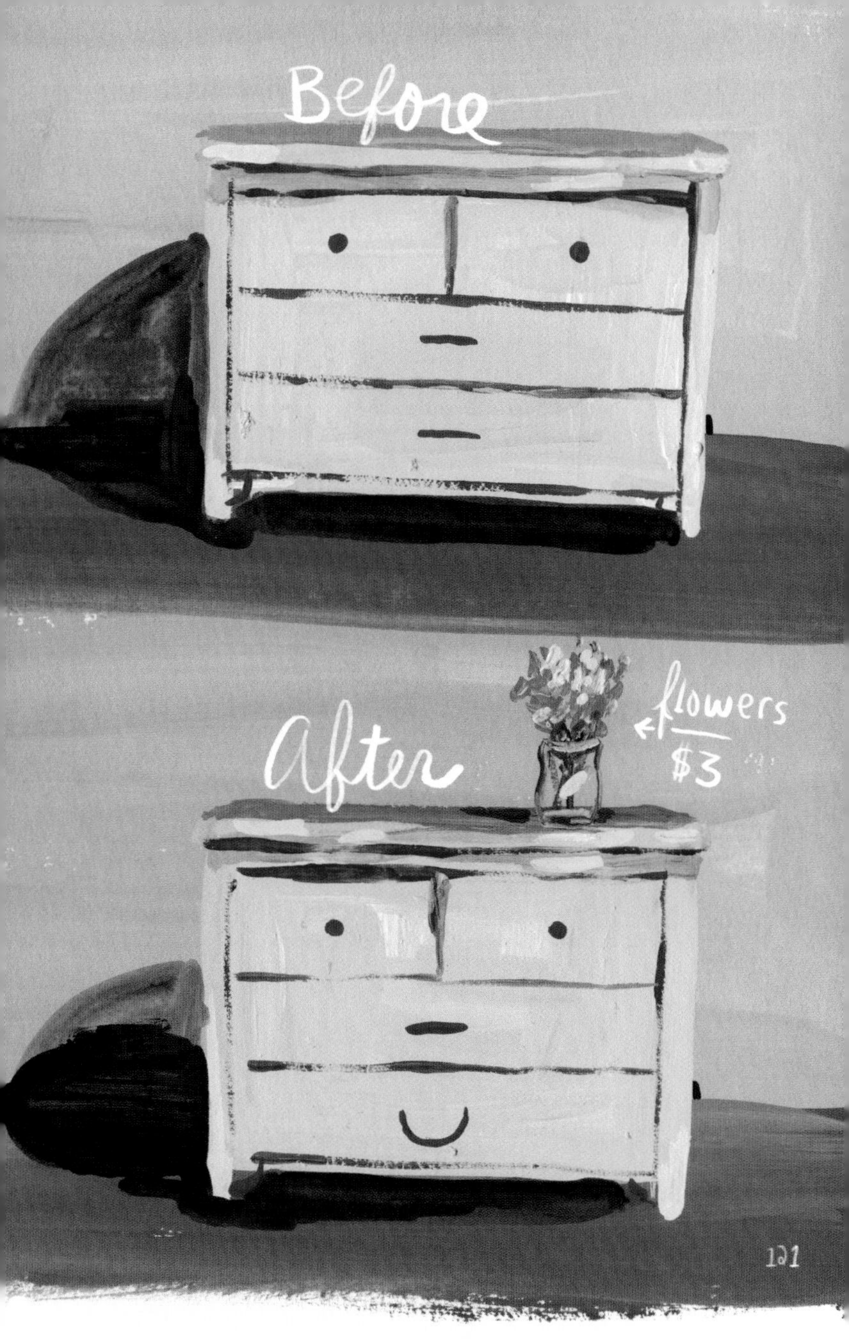
Before
After
flowers
$3

Tiny improvements to hearth and wardrobe bring little bleeps of joy that can last for ages. When my husband hangs a picture in a new spot, I can enjoy looking at that wall in a charmed light for months.

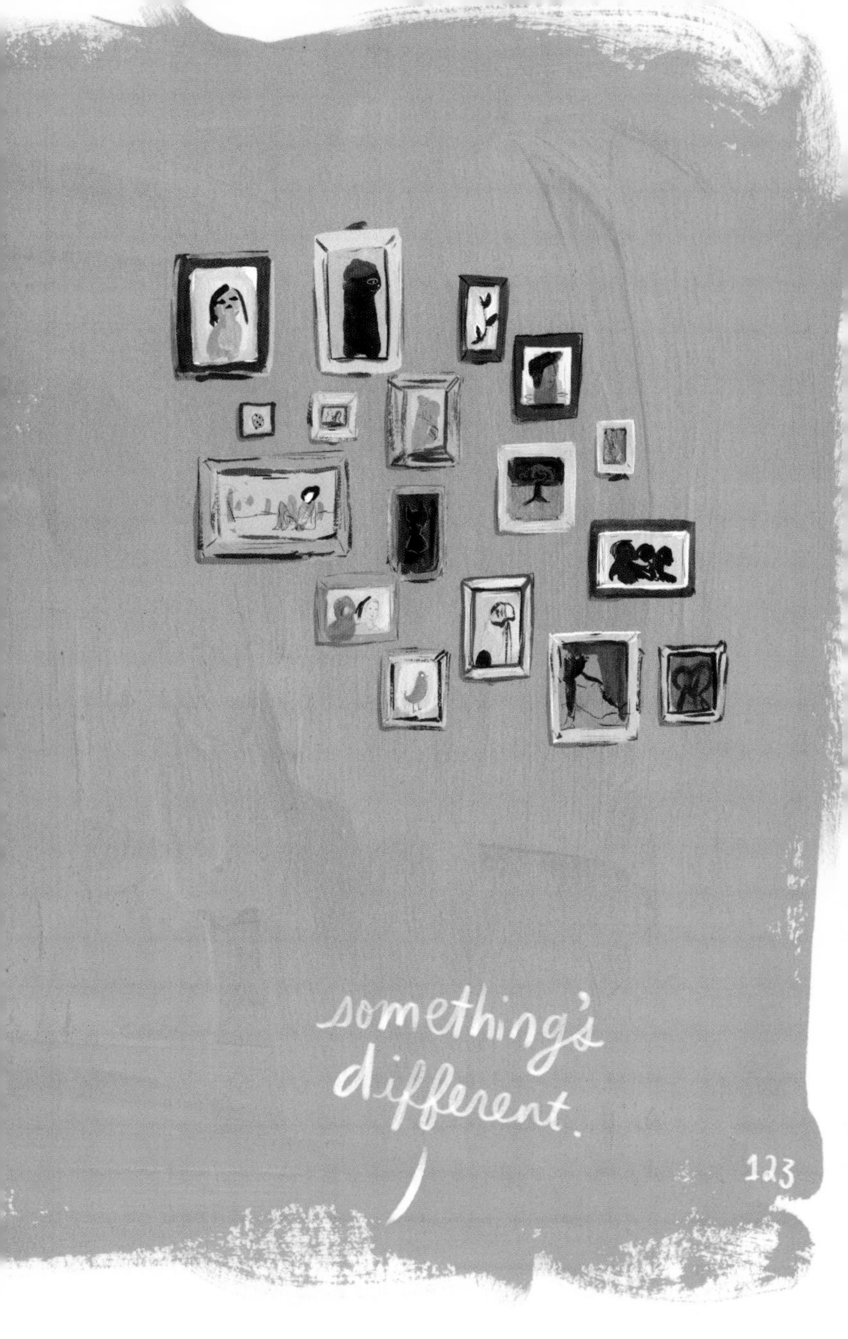
something's
different.

Kaizen is the Japanese theory of slow, gradual improvement. Over the years my husband and I have become proponents of it, undoubtedly bastardizing the philosophy as we fashion our own joyful little mode of slow home improvement. Since we can't afford to tackle the huge stuff ("Rip off the entire back of your house," suggested an architect), we fix our house in fits and starts. And though we're both less handy than a dog wearing a tool belt, we continually manage to make things better.

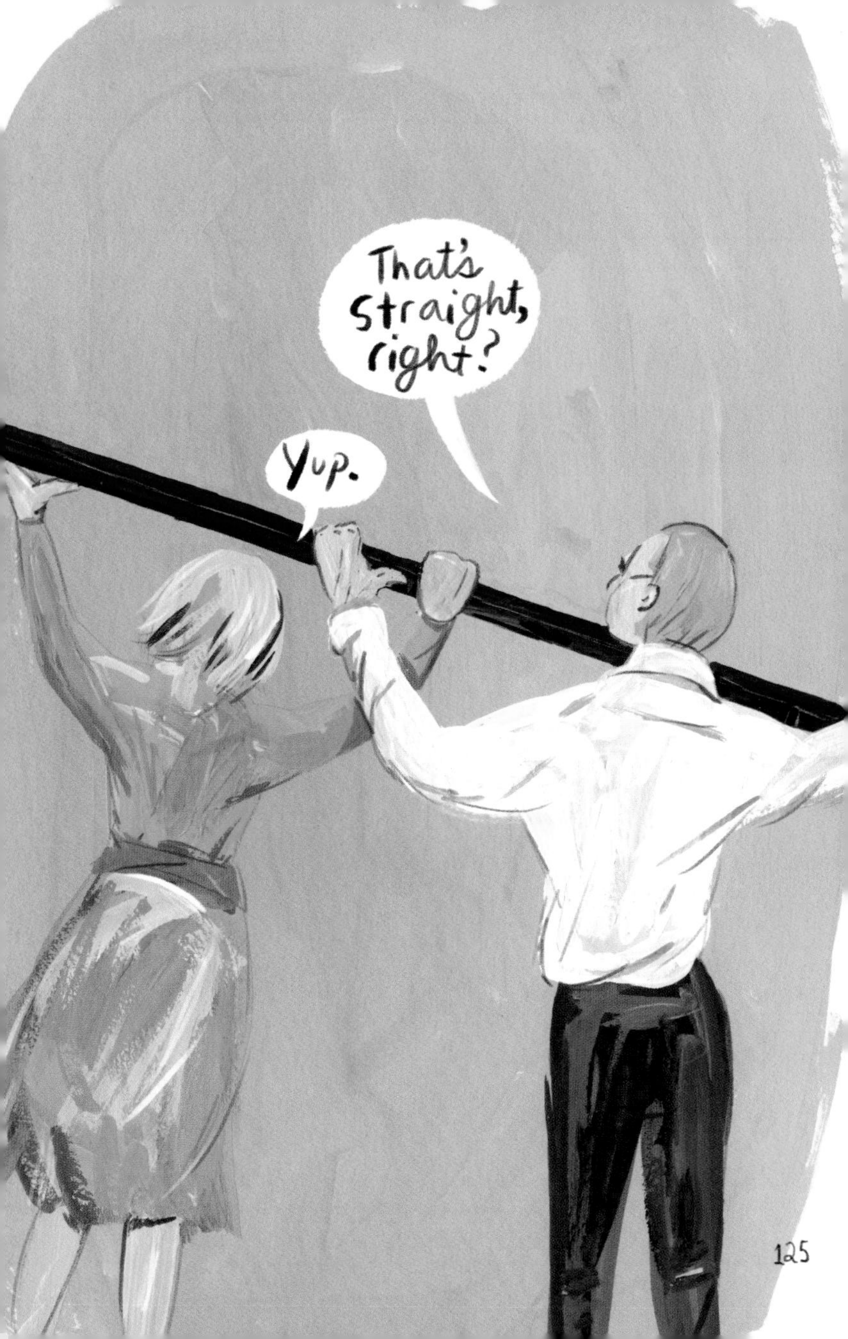
That's straight, right?
Yup.

When I visit a house that has been lovingly lived in for years, I often find it has a cozy utility. Time has enabled the implementation of peak efficiency— the coffee table at just the right angle, the reading lamp that glows warm and perfect, the spices at eye level. It's why experts say you should live in a space for a few years before renovating.

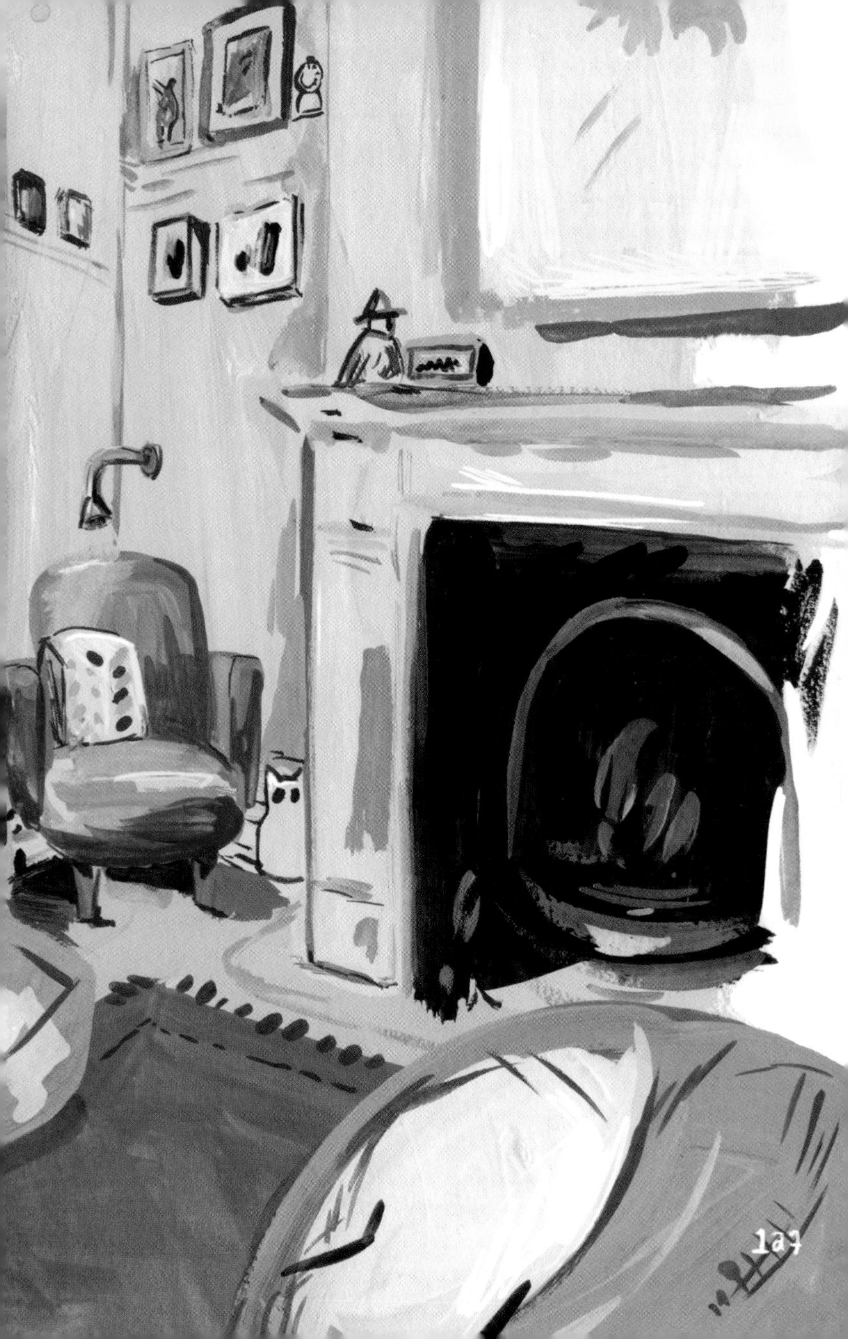

Which makes sense. If it takes me a week of thoughtful deliberation to figure out which winter boots to buy, it ought to take a commensurate amount of time to decide what kind of kitchen table I want to have for the rest of my life.

LEGS too fat

NO glass

TOO SQUARE

WILL BARN BOARD BE LAUGHABLE IN TWO YEARS?

TOO OVULAR? (IS OVULAR a word?)

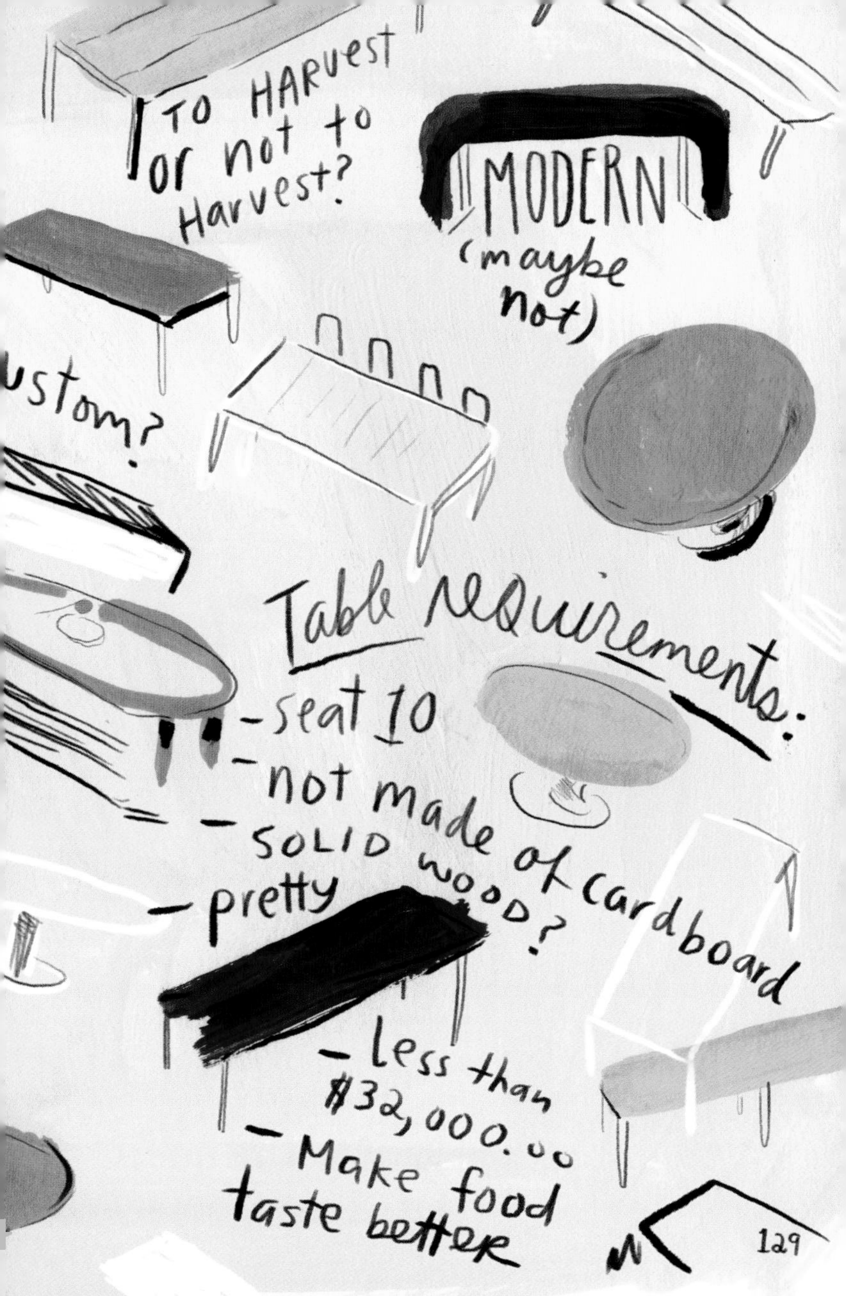

TO HARVEST or not to Harvest?
MODERN (maybe not)
ustom?
Table requirements:
- seat 10
- not made of cardboard
- SOLID WOOD?
- pretty
- less than $32,000.00
- Make food taste better

Is it simplistic to reduce the problem of consumption to a matter of slowing down? Yes. But it's idiotic to shop at warp speed, as I used to. I blame a childhood spent watching *Supermarket Sweep*.

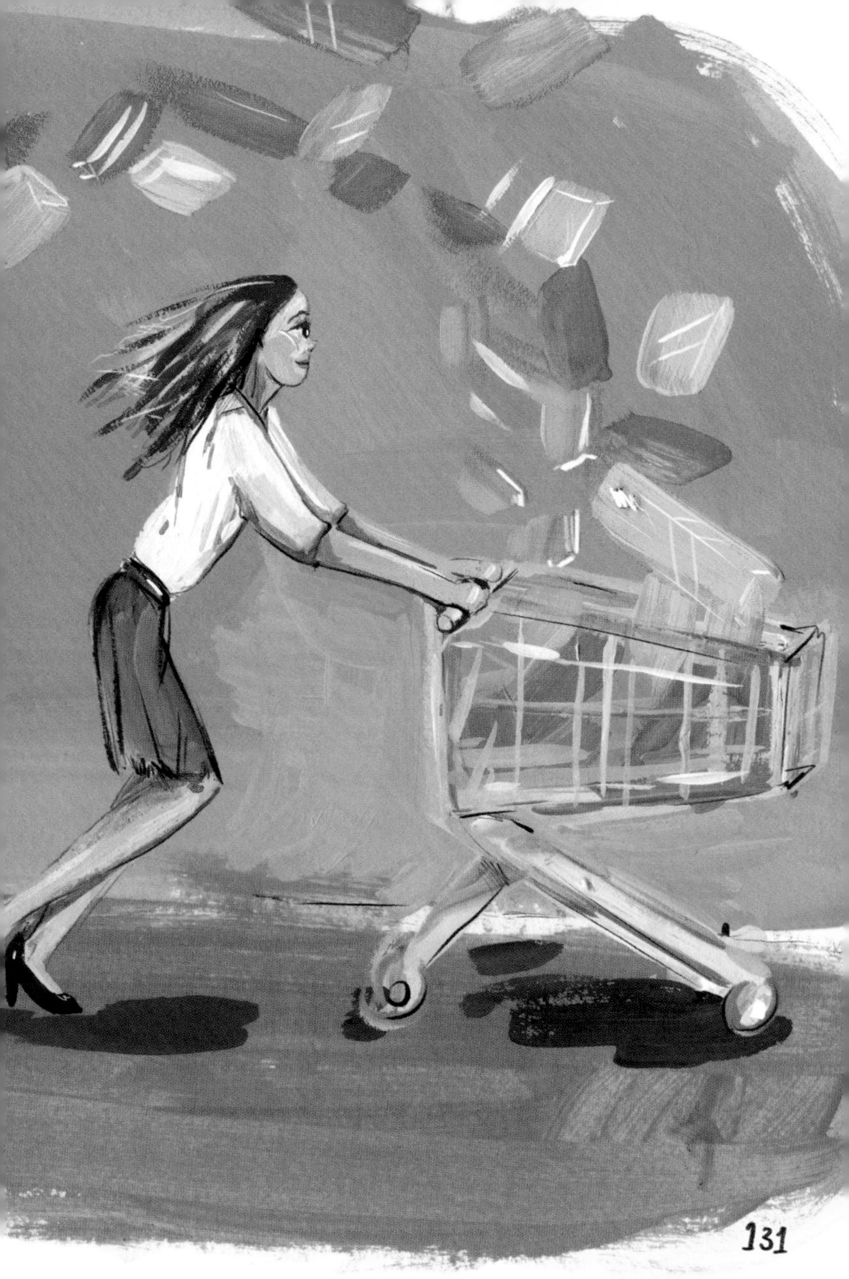

Also, *slow* is so often a pejorative, both because speedy productivity is the game of the day and because the slow-food movement has a frisson of twee about it. This is too bad, because slow shopping is a big part of the answer.

Slow and sustainable dress (available in snail, turtle, and molasses)

Of course, the impulse to beautify one's space is exacerbated by the voyeurism that bloggy "house tours" and Instagrammed living rooms enable. It's never been easier to see how the other whole lives.

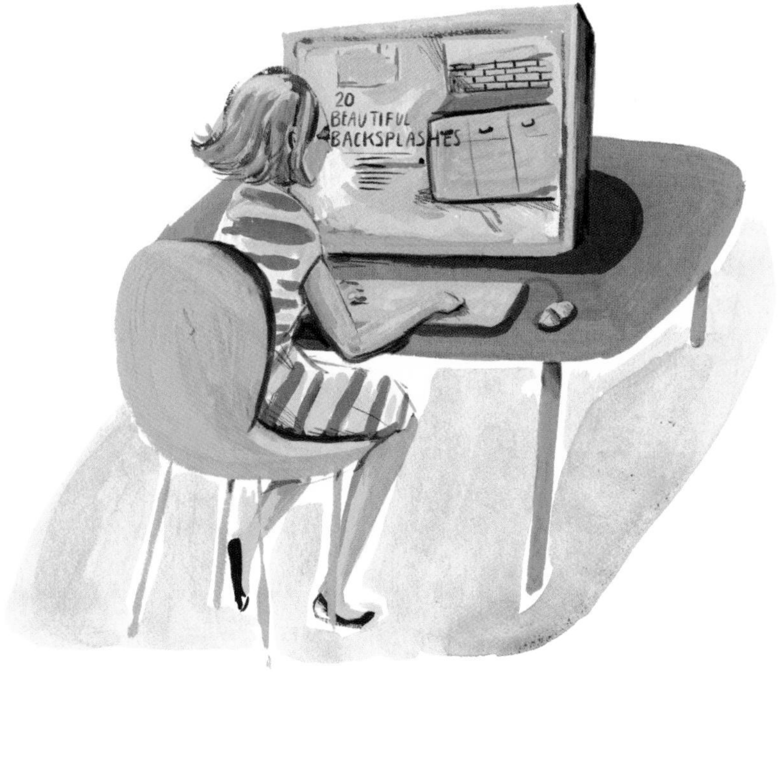
20
BEAUTIFUL
BACKSPLASHES

One of my favorite online magazines is called *Covet Garden*, which, though I love a pun, is kind of a gross name. Shouldn't we be embarrassed to say we covet stuff? Isn't it the word that follows "Thou shalt not"? Another website called *The Coveteur* invites fancy people to shamelessly show us all the expensive things they've bought. While *Covet Garden* is Marimekko cute, *The Coveteur* is Versace vulgar. But it's all on a covet continuum.

CONTINUUM of DESIRE

Swarovski	—	wasteful
Versace	—	Blingy
Forever 21	—	Bingey
bebe	—	Showy
Claire's	—	Frivolous
H&M	—	Indulgent
Etsy	—	Quirky
Gap	—	Average
Lands' END	—	Modest
L.L.Bean	—	Judicious
Sears	—	Frugal
Goodwill	—	Penny-pinchy
Burlap sacks	—	Abstemious
Nothing	—	Off-grid

So,   SLOW

138

I   go.

In my effort to reconcile beauty and thrift, there's a fear of becoming preoccupied with thoughtful consumption. It's this aversion to letting the banality of buying take up time in one's life that makes avowed shopping haters out of so many of us. But that's because we've long thought of shopping as frivolous leisure, when in truth it is real work.

TIP
Take frequent naps to keep your strength up.

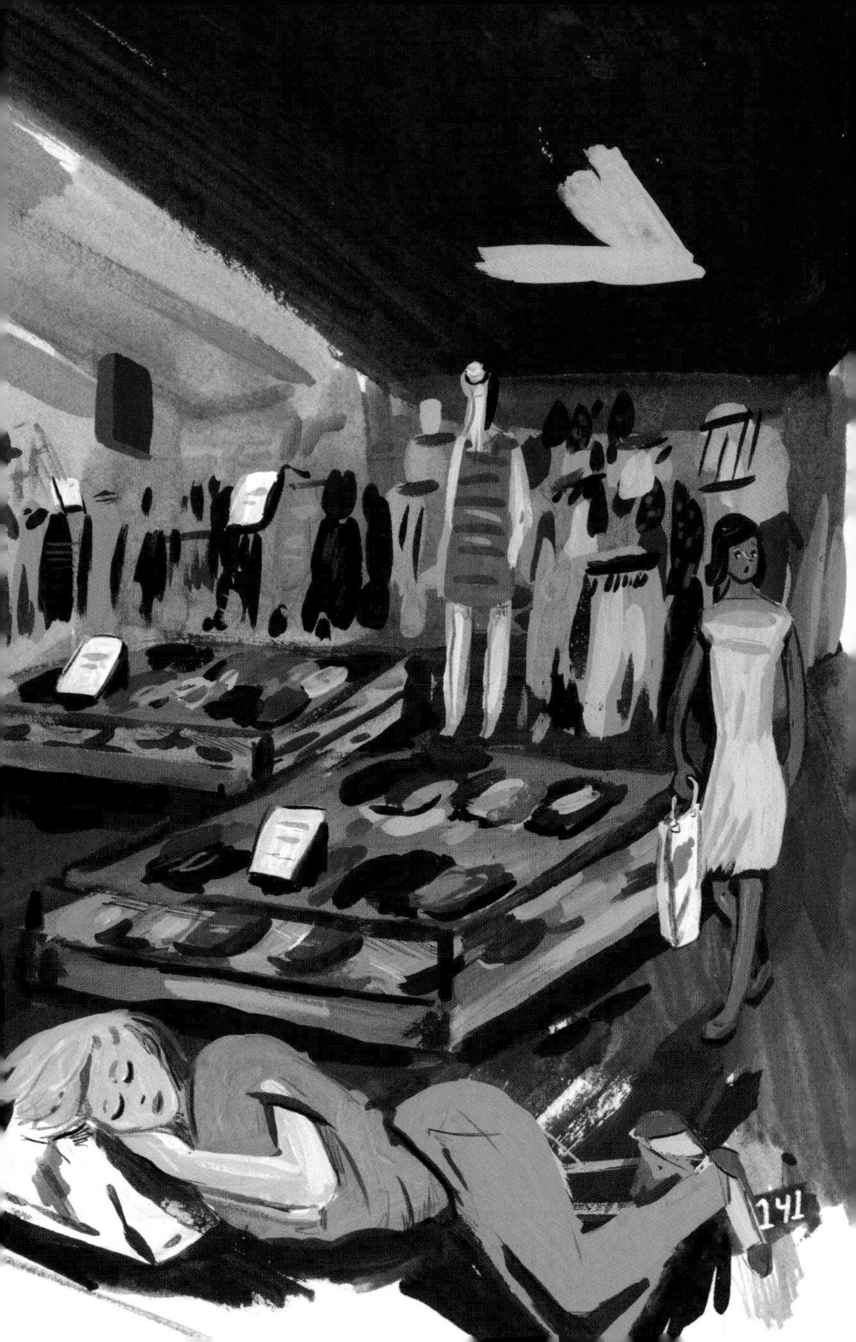

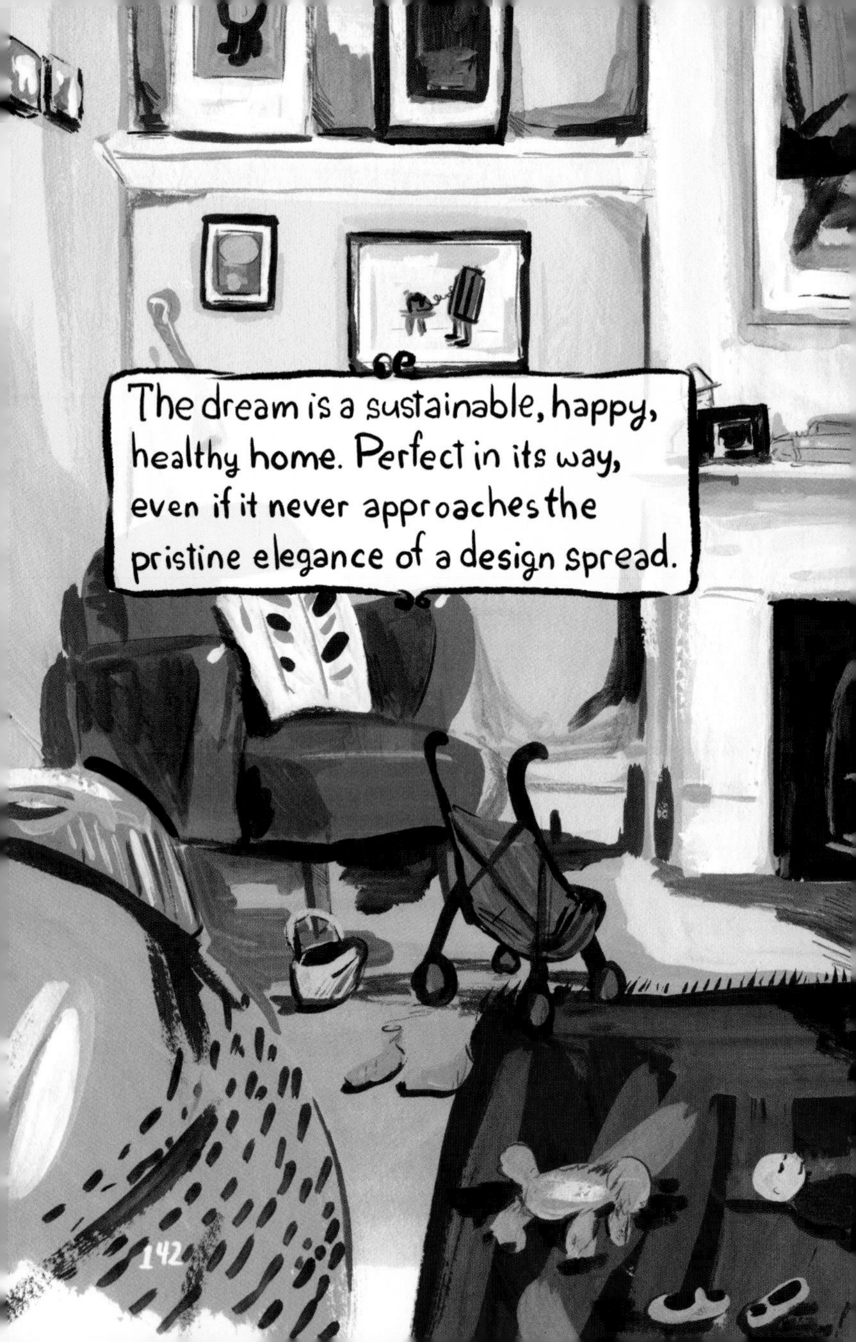
The dream is a sustainable, happy, healthy home. Perfect in its way, even if it never approaches the pristine elegance of a design spread.

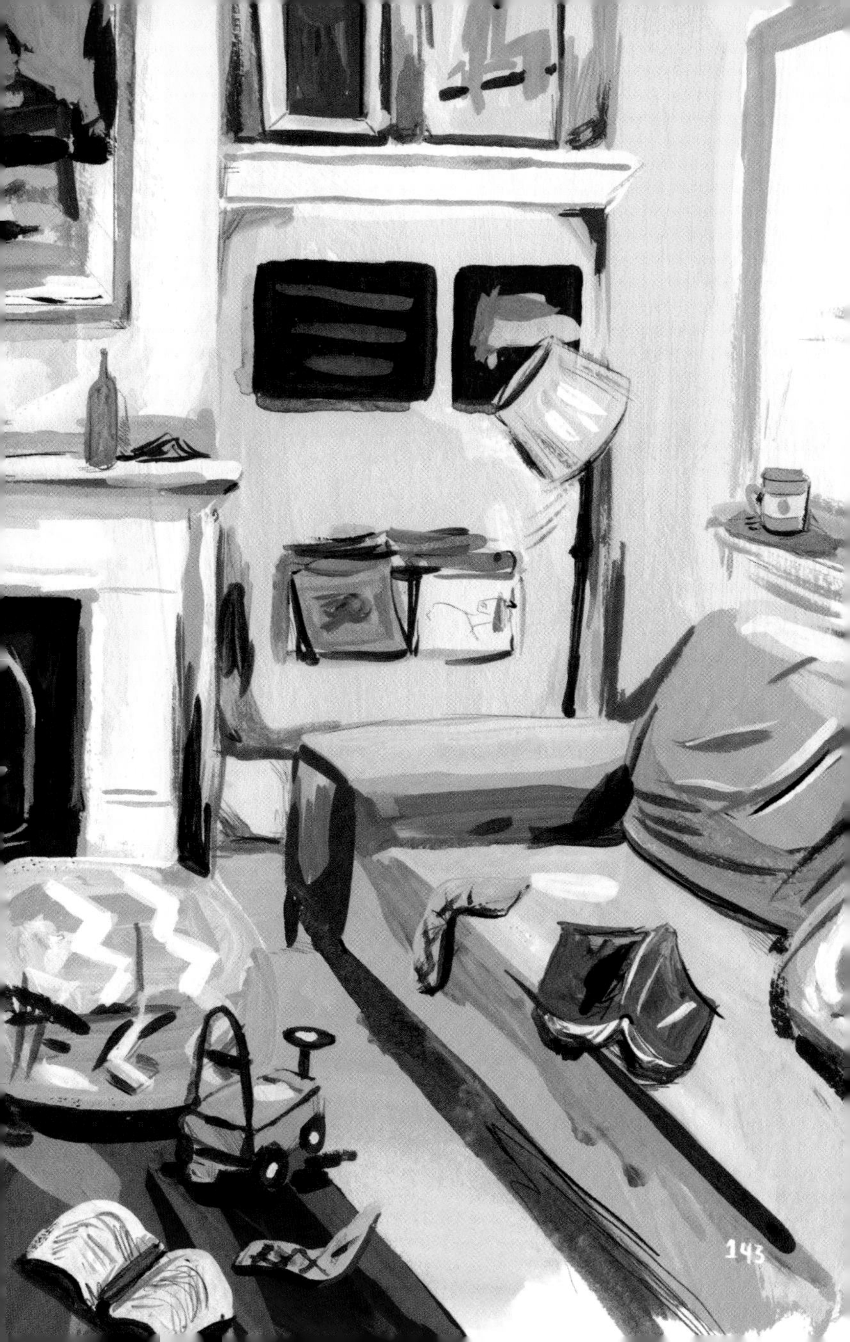

Chapter Seven

CONCLUSIONS

A GRAB BAG of STUFF, including:

- A very short guide to quality
- Simple rules for better shopping
- Quick tips and best practices
- Important scientific charts
- An Illustrated bibliography
- A glossary of terms
- Collaborative consumption
- Impact statement
- ~~The meaning of life~~
- Good vibes

So where does
all this consumer research
leave me?
Without a perfect
answer.

But with a well-
established
protocol for how to
(NOT) shop.
I'M slow, steady, and
intent on quality.
I'm strong enough to
eye the mint-green brogues
and know I won't buy them.
What I love best is how time
often reveals a solution to
what I need that
doesn't involve buying.

146

The following pages include facts, tips, and loose rules to help you establish your own shopping strategies.

A VERY SHORT GUIDE TO
QUALITY

You could spend a lifetime studying quality. It can be harder to pin down than a toddler in an ice cream shop. Where once you could rely upon certain brands for consistent quality, these days it's best to parse it piece by piece. A high price doesn't guarantee good quality, and a low price doesn't eliminate it. What's a shopper to do?

The designer Katya Revenko takes a holistic approach. "First, examine the design. Is it a style that you love? That's lasting and not too trendy?" Only then do you begin to examine fit and finish—the draping, seam, stitching, and details that give you insight into how the garment will wear.

BUT, it's a compromise. You wouldn't buy a limousine to haul garbage to the dump. And you wouldn't buy a silk jumpsuit to take a cardio-funk class. Not that anybody should ever take a cardio-funk class.

FEEL

NATURAL fibers tend to be nicer than man-made, but both have a place.

NATURAL	**MAN-MADE**
cotton	Rayon
wool	Nylon
cashmere	Polyester
	Kardashian

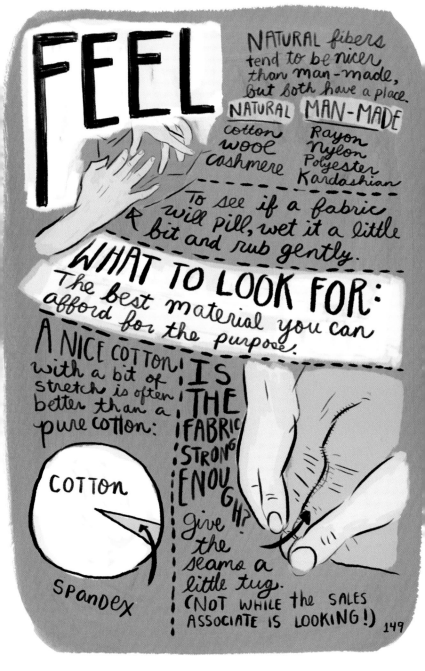

To see if a fabric will pill, wet it a little bit and rub gently.

WHAT TO LOOK FOR:

The best material you can afford for the purpose.

A NICE COTTON with a bit of stretch is often better than a pure cotton:

COTTON

SPANDEX

IS THE FABRIC STRONG ENOUGH? give the seams a little tug. (NOT WHILE the SALES ASSOCIATE IS LOOKING!)

CUT

CHEAPER garments have less generous cuts. This means they usually feel SKIMPIER. There's LESS seam allowance and LESS hem allowance, and the garment can sometimes feel PINCHED in places.

EASE

Refers to the amount of extra fabric in a piece. (NOT HOW BIG the garment actually is!)

A good cut hangs well and lets you BREATHE. (Unless it's specifically tailored to not let you breathe!)

GEOMETRIC   SCHLUMPY

TASTE

While some people like really structured cuts, others like less tailored garments.

It's the little details that tell you much about a piece. And it's what's inside that counts, too. THINK ABOUT:

- SEAMS
- LINING
- BIAS
- BUTTONS
- TRIM
- STITCHING

GOOD

NOT SO GOOD

BUTTONS

Are they of good quality? (NOT PLASTIC)

ARE THEY sturdy? ARE THEY sewn on WELL?

IS THERE A SHANK?

COAT BUTTONS SHOULD HAVE A REINFORCEMENT BUTTON ON THE INSIDE.

BUTTON HOLES

Are they properly Stitched?

Finish

STITCHING

IS THE STITCHING SOLID? STRAIGHT? PRETTY?

ZIPPERS

SHOULD HAVE GOOD TEETH AND BE PROPERLY SEWN INTO THE GARMENT.

SEQUINS, Lace, & TRIM SHOULD BE NEAT.

POCKETS

Is the pocket lined? Is it well crafted? Can you fit a large chocolate bar in it?

SIMPLE RULES for BETTER SHOPPING
RULE #1

In *The Beauty Experiment*, Phoebe Baker Hyde makes the case for seven years as the goal for how long an item should last. Aim for seven years, hope for ten.

Camper boots I bought in 2008 and still love. (The militant equestrian look was already out of style when I bought them.)

RULE #2

People who say you should get rid of one item of clothing for every item you take in should be tickled to death with a polyester boa. I invariably come back to pieces I thought I'd completely tired of. Life is an endless cycle of hating and loving tapered ankles. That said, if you never wear something, pass it on.

Bell-bottoms!   Bell-bottoms.   Bell-bottoms!

2006   2009   2013

RULE#3

Don't buy anything the first time you see it unless it's the thing you've been searching for all your life and it is flying by on a speeding train, never to be seen again. Even then, don't buy it.

(You will never find a satchel like this again, and you will dream about it for ~~years~~ decades. And then you'll forget about it.)

RULE #4
Never buy anything just because it's on sale.

3-sleeve shirt, $149.99 sale! $9.99

RULE #5

When you really want something new, find the thing in your closet that comes closest to it. If they are closer than a clog's length apart, don't buy the new thing.

in my

CLOSET

what I

COVET

RULE #6

Conscious consumerism is not an excuse to shop. It may be a fair-trade, organic leg warmer, but if your legs aren't cold, it's still a frivolous purchase.

But they have built-in SPF!

QUICK TIPS

When you really want a new pair of shoes, put on a favorite pair that you don't get to wear often enough. Caress them in an almost creepy fashion. (Ew.)

Take a sewing class so you can mend and tweak old items.

Really inspect the detailing on one of your finest pieces of clothing. Hold all subsequent purchases up to that standard.

Make a list of things you really want and a list of things you really need. Things that appear on both lists take precedence.

WANT
feather Boa
Chia Pet
Lava lamp
NEED
socks
broom

slow down

Stop 🛒 Cart ▾ window-shopping on the Internet.

Stuff doesn't make you hot. You're hottest with no stuff at all.

Best Practices

SLOWING
PERSONAL
CONSUMPTION

REWORKING
ENTIRE
WORLD
ECONOMY

Whether or not I buy this sweater won't change much. Whether or not this sweater is ethically produced won't change much either. But establishing a thoughtful and informed means of consuming is a fundamental part of understanding how significant the bigger issues of resource management are. Not shopping is but one sleeve of the sustainability sweater. Which, by the way, is really cute and cozy, and comes with a lifetime guarantee.

159

THE BUYERARCHY
of NEEDS
(with apologies to
Maslow)

Do the RIGHT Things

THINGS
I need

THINGS
I WANT

THINGS I BUY

THINGS
I USE

THINGS
PEOPLE WHO
DON'T KNOW
ME THAT WELL
give me

CRAP

THINGS
THAT
MAGICALLY
MATERIALIZE
in my
HOUSE

ANNOTATED

A CHEATER'S GUIDE to SOME OF THE GREAT WRITING OUT THERE

"Clothes are so cheap today that buying them often feels inconsequential."
— Elizabeth L. Cline, *Overdressed: The Shockingly High Cost of Cheap Fashion*

LATTe $4.99   Dress $4.99

"Shopping for things I need isn't leisure; it's a task, just like many others. And shopping for things don't need yields buying things I don't need. (Plus a headache.)" — Phoebe Baker Hyde, *The Beauty Experiment*

RETAIL

THERAPY

"Buying, lots of buying, was the antidote for what plagued modern existence: the anonymity of city life, the tedium of the workplace, the loss of individuality brought on by the growth of impersonal corporations."
— Lee Eisenberg, *Shoptimism: Why the American Consumer Will Keep On Buying No Matter What*

"'Thingness' being that quality or qualities that gives an item 'attitude.'"
— Lee Eisenberg, *Shoptimism: Why the American Consumer Will Keep On Buying No Matter What*

What is it?   A Thing.

BIBLIOGRAPHY

Quality

"There used to be more of a direct connection between high-end clothing and quality. Now a designer name is no guarantee of craftsmanship. As early as 1994, *Consumer Reports* was finding that designer clothing at Barneys, in the case of a rayon chenille sweater, often offered no better quality than Kmart." —Elizabeth L. Cline, *Overdressed: The Shockingly High Cost of Cheap Fashion*, citing information from *The End of Fashion*, by Teri Agins

"Every year, Americans throw away 12.7 million tons, or 68 pounds of textiles per person, according to the EPA, which also estimates that 1.6 million tons of this waste could be recycled or reused." —Elizabeth L. Cline, *Overdressed: The Shockingly High Cost of Cheap Fashion*

"Successfully situated in homey space, the occupant of homey space becomes a homey creature. He or she appears to take on the properties of the surrounding space and objects. A kind of meaning transfer has been achieved." —Grant McCracken, "Homeyness: A Cultural Account of One Constellation of Consumer Goods and Meanings"

THINGS WITH SPARKLES

"As a social phenomenon, it's always seemed to me that consumerism occurs along two dimensions: a vertical one, in which consumption is a scoreboard for achievement or status, and a horizontal one, in which it's a medium for personal expression." —Bruce Philp, *Consumer Republic*

ANNOTATED

"The clothes you put on do not instantly make you the character you want to be. Clothes are a lifelong journey into acquiring an identity, an identity deliberately formulated, but also made by accident. You try on a tweed jacket and understand that it has connected with the part of yourself you scarcely knew about, which would like to go for a walk along a country road, with dogs. Or you put on a hat and discover in yourself a capacity to be quite lah-di-dah." - Linda Grant, *The Thoughtful Dresser*

"What I question is not consumption in the abstract but consumerism and overconsumption. While consumption means acquiring and using goods and services to meet one's needs, consumerism is the particular relationship to consumption in which we seek to meet our emotional and social needs through shopping, and we define and demonstrate our self-worth through the Stuff we own. And overconsumption is when we take far more resources than we need and than the planet can sustain, as is the case in most of the United States as well as a growing number of other countries."*

"Trying to consume our way out of the mess we're in is a familiar dead end. Many people believe or hope that if we just buy greener, if we buy this instead of that, everything will be OK. Sorry to be a buzzkill here, but we need way more than that. . . . Skeptics call this concept 'greensumption,' while advocates call it 'conscious consuming.'"*

BIBLIOGRAPHY

"Simplicity is a lighter lifestyle that fits elegantly into the real world of the twenty-first century."
–Duane Elgin, *Voluntary Simplicity*

"Luxury is not consumerism. It is educating the eyes to see that special quality."
–Christian Louboutin in *Deluxe: How Luxury Lost Its Luster*, by Dana Thomas

HAPPINESS

"Transforming our levels and patterns of consumption requires our looking directly into how we create our sense of identity and seek our happiness."
–Duane Elgin, *Voluntary Simplicity*

"Buy clothes. Not too many. Mostly quality."
–Me, with thanks to Michael Pollan

165

A glossary of terms

VEBLEN goods

Goods for which desire rises in tandem with their price, as higher price confers status. Named after Thorstein Veblen, who coined the term *conspicuous consumption*, which is defined as "acquiring luxury goods to display power and status."

THORSTEIN VEBLEN

CONSPICUOUS CONSUMP-TION

greige goods

"These are partially prepped and assembled pieces produced overseas in the lowest-wage factories (think undyed fabric roughly precut for sleeves or torsos but not yet sewn together). Greige goods are shipped to factories close to the retail stores to be finalized, which could mean being given the neckline or sleeve length or specific color that consumers are snapping up that week." —Annie Leonard, *The Story of Stuff*

PLANNED OBSOLESCENCE

The practice of designing a product with a limited shelf life so that it ceases to function after a certain amount of time.

THIS BELT WILL SELF-DESTRUCT *in five wears!*

DIDEROT EFFECT

I just feel so shabby now.

When the acquisition of a high-end material good inspires the increased consumption of equally high-end materials.

PRODUCT stewardship, OR PRODUCER RESPONSIBILITY

RETURN to SENDER

The idea that companies should be held financially responsible for the life of their products, from care to recycling to disposal.

167

Collaborative

The idea is that we share things instead of individually owning them. This makes sense for hedge trimmers, food dehydrators, and bouncy castles. It also makes sense for fright wigs, prom dresses, and go-go boots. Unless you wear your go-go boots every day.

The problem is that in an age of buy buy buy for cheap cheap cheap, it seems easier to buy the $9.99 fright wig instead of borrowing it. If it's ours we're less stressed about damaging it, losing it, or scaring it away. But even if it's more taxing to borrow than buy, share we must, as the world has a limited supply of go-go boots.

And yet we're out of sharing practice. Which means we often need to be reminded to return things neatly, promptly, and gratefully—with a bottle of wine, if the loan in question is a biggie. That's all there is to it.

Consumption

HOW TO BORROW:

- ASK NICELY
- TAKE good CARE
- RETURN cleanly AND promptly
- Reciprocate

- -

START a sharing community with friends, neighbors, or extremely fashionable strangers. Someone will want to borrow your _____.

Impact Statement

A trillion adorable artisanal baby trees were cruelly slaughtered to make the paper this book was printed on. How can I reconcile such murder with the practices I'm trying to espouse herein? I'm not sure.

Why do creative works get a free pass when it comes to sustainability? Because life would be horrid without them. At the same time, my philosophy is to go about even my arty pursuits with a mind toward economy of resources.*

Also, if you plant this book in your backyard, a tree will grow.

If you LIKE something, PASS It on!

*Economy of resources: Don't forgo doing wonderful things, but use as little as you need to get the job done.

AND ONE FINAL THING:

YOU LOOK AMAZING

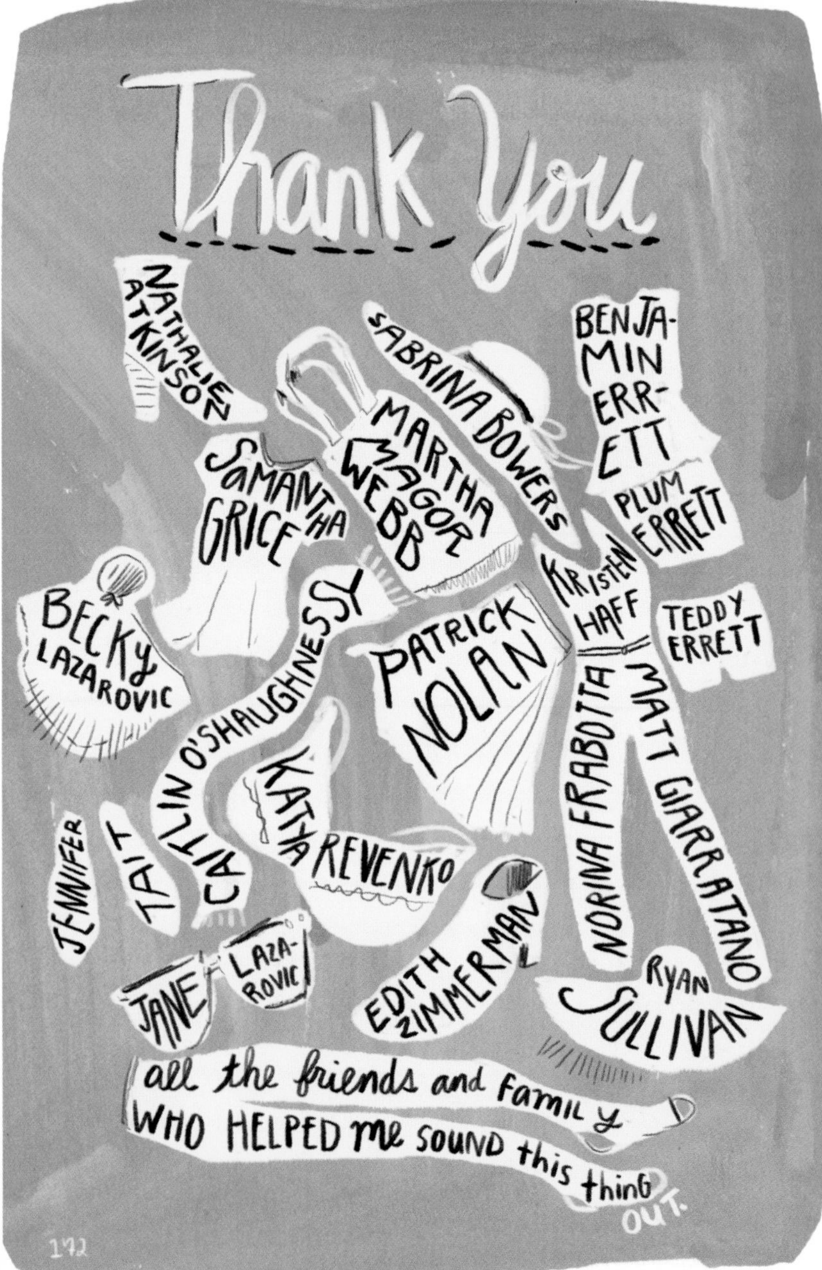
Thank You
NATHALIE ATKINSON
SABRINA BOWERS
BENJAMIN ERRETT
MARTHA MAGOR WEBB
SAMANTHA GRICE
PLUM ERRETT
BECKY LAZAROVIC
KRISTEN HAFF
TEDDY ERRETT
PATRICK NOLAN
CAITLIN O'SHAUGHNESSY
NORINA FRABOTTA
MATT GIARRATANO
KATYA REVENKO
JENNIFER TAIT
EDITH ZIMMERMAN
JANE LAZAROVIC
RYAN SULLIVAN
all the friends and family WHO HELPED me SOUND this thing OUT.

A page of this book that you can write on!

NOW, is there something you really want?
Is it useful? ☐
Well-made? ☐
Wonderful? ☐

What is it:

> Draw, paint, or describe item in rhyming verse:
>
> Date: _____

Come back to this spot in one year.
Does it still make your heart beat faster? ☐ ←

If you checked this box: a) get your heart examined. B) allow yourself to purchase said item.

This book is now over.
I know. I'm sad, too.
But we can still hang out
together at:

A Bunch of
Pretty.com

Meet me there!